HOW TO SPEAK AT SPECIAL EVENTS

How to Speak
at Special Events

CHRISTIAN
FOCUS

ISBN 1-84550-277-9
ISBN 978-1-84550-277-5

© Sydney Missionary and Bible College

10 9 8 7 6 5 4 3 2 1

Previously published in 2003 by SMBC Press
with the title *How to Prepare a Bible Talk*

Published in 2007
by
Christian Focus Publications,
Geanies House, Fearn, Ross-shire,
IV20 1TW, Scotland, UK

www.christianfocus.com

Cover design by Moose77.com

Printed and bound by CPD, Wales

Contents

FOREWORD

The book you are holding has been written by 14 different authors with one common purpose: to equip you to prepare a talk from the Bible that provides a clear explanation of what the text says, and how it applies to the life of your listeners.

It is important to note that all of the authors have prepared their own chapters independent of one another.

Our target audience is not the theologically trained pastor, but the person in the pew who is called on to preach occasionally, or who takes a turn on the roster to speak at Youth Group or lead the Bible study group.

We have tried to provide the equipment to present Bible talks to all sorts of groups in all sorts of settings.

All of the authors are practitioners and I am grateful for their willingness to contribute their insights into this book. I trust you will find it really helpful as you prepare your next Bible talk.

Thanks to Otto Peeters, missionary pilot, and good friend, who saw the need for a book like this and who initiated this project.

Special thanks from all of the authors to Sarah Buckle-Dykes for her editorial contribution, which makes us read better than we are able to write.

David Cook

Section 1

Preparing Yourself

1.

PREACHING: A DEFINITION

SAM CHAN

Our Christian meetings focus upon preaching. The Bible also speaks a lot about preaching. Most of the Bible's major characters were preachers. Poor old Jonah once ended up in the belly of a fish because he had tried to get himself off the preaching roster. And preaching has also been a key feature in the history of the Christian church. George Whitefield (1714–1770), the English evangelist, sometimes preached thirteen sermons in one week and to crowds as large as 100,000.

I have been asked to provide a definition of preaching as a foundation for the rest of this book. But how should we define preaching? Should it be defined by its method? I was once invited to preach to a youth group on a Friday night. The organisers had creatively set up the night with an unconventional programme of film, drama, interviews, loud music and games. When it was my turn to preach I thought that I would reciprocate with an equally creative unconventional sermon. Afterwards, the organisers told me how disappointed they were because I had failed to 'preach the Bible'. Maybe they thought that unless I preached a Sunday 'three-point' sermon, which followed a Bible passage 'verse-by-verse', I had failed to 'preach the Bible'?

When I was studying at Sydney Missionary and Bible College, one of our fellow-students had a PhD in education and he would try out his latest theories in our preaching workshops. When he preached, he would dazzle us with a combination of preaching, singing and computer slide-shows. He certainly had our attention, but we were never sure how to critique his sermons. I would still argue that he had faithfully 'preached the Bible'.

The Bible hardly restricts us to only one method of preaching. The Old Testament prophets sometimes preached in oracles and sometimes acted out their message. The apostles changed their style of preaching according to their audiences and settings. Jesus sometimes preached a formal sermon and sometimes preached in puzzling parables. I don't think Jesus would ever have scored well in one of our contemporary preaching workshops. In fact, I'm not sure where we would even find a three-point verse-by-verse sermon in the Bible. So perhaps we are heading in the wrong direction if we try to define preaching by a method.

Instead, our aim will be to provide a theological definition of preaching. Our method will be to begin with a suggested definition, survey how this is supported by the Bible's storylines own presentation of preaching, and then come to a conclusion.

A definition of preaching

Preaching is a joint activity between God and the preacher: God speaking his Word, through the human proclamation of God's Word, which the Spirit applies to the hearer.

Survey of the Bible's storyline

Our definition of preaching contains three parts. We will now support each of these parts by surveying the presentation of preaching in the Bible's storyline.

1. God speaks his Word

God reveals himself to us in many ways, one of which is through his speech, that is, God speaks his Word to us. This is a foundational concept of the Bible. Phrases such as 'this is what the LORD says', 'God said', 'the LORD has spoken', and 'the Word of the LORD' occur over and over again in the Bible.

A few years ago the Tickle-Me-Elmo doll was the 'in thing'. My parents bought one and, sure enough, if you tickled Elmo, he would squirm and squeal. That is, until the batteries died. Then Elmo just sat there and said nothing. Idols and false gods are like a Tickle-Me-Elmo with dead batteries. They don't do or say anything. Instead they sit, collect dust and can be sold for $2 at a garage sale.

In contrast, God is the God who speaks his Word. He is the speaking God. On the first page of the Bible, God speaks the heavens and earth into existence. At both Jesus' baptism and transfiguration, God speaks, 'This is my Son, whom I love. Listen to him'. And on the Bible's last page, God speaks from his throne in heaven.

But how does God speak his Word to us? In the Bible, God speaks through a variety of methods, sometimes through dreams, visions, angels, a voice and even a donkey. But in addition to all these, God often speaks through human messengers or proclaimers – especially the prophets in the Old Testament and Jesus, the apostles and the Christian church in the New Testament. The writer of Hebrews sums this up for us: 'In the past God spoke to our forefathers through the prophets at many times and in various ways, but in these last days he has spoken to us by his Son...' (Heb. 1:1-2).

The Bible affirms that God does speak through his human messengers. These messengers are speaking God's Word. For example, when the prophet Nathan conveys God's promise of an everlasting covenant to King David (2 Sam. 7:4-17), David responds by identifying Nathan's message as God's own words (2 Sam. 7:28). Later, King Solomon looks back to Nathan's message and declares, 'And now, O God of Israel, let your word that you promised your servant David my father come true' (1 Kings 8:26; 2 Chron. 6:16). Solomon also identifies Nathan's message as God's own words.

Therefore, in this brief survey of the Bible, we can say that God is a God who speaks his Word to us, and one way is through his messengers or proclaimers.

2. The human proclaims God's Word

What makes someone a proclaimer of God's Word? There are four important criteria: they are commissioned by God; they are anointed by the Spirit; they receive their words from God; and they faithfully proclaim God's Word.

The life and ministry of Moses exemplify these four criteria. Firstly, Moses is commissioned by God. In Exodus 3, God appears to Moses and commissions him to be his prophet:

> God said to Moses, 'I AM WHO I AM. This is what you are to say to the Israelites: "I AM has sent me to you"'.

> God also said to Moses, 'Say to the Israelites, "The LORD, the God of your fathers – the God of Abraham, the God of Isaac and the God of Jacob – has sent me to you"' (Exod. 3:14-15a).

As someone commissioned by God, Moses speaks on God's behalf and his words have the same authority as God's words.

Secondly, Moses is anointed by the Spirit. We learn this from the following narrative:

> Then the LORD came down in the cloud and spoke with [Moses], and he took of the Spirit that was on him and put the Spirit on the seventy elders. When the Spirit rested on them, they prophesied, but they did not do so again (Num. 11:25).

The Spirit authors God's words and empowers Moses and the other prophets to 'prophesy', that is, to speak God's words. But without the Spirit, it is impossible for anyone to speak God's words.

Thirdly, Moses receives his words from God. After Moses receives his commission in Exodus 3, he hesitates to go because he is not 'eloquent' (Exod. 4:10). As a result, the LORD replies:

> 'Who gave man his mouth? ... Is it not I, the LORD? Now go; I will help you speak and will teach you what to say.' But Moses said, "O Lord, please send someone else to do

it.' Then the LORD's anger burned against Moses and he said, 'What about your brother, Aaron the Levite? ... You shall speak to him and put words in his mouth; I will help both of you speak and will teach you what to do. He will speak to the people for you, and it will be as if he were your mouth and as if you were God to him' (Exod. 4:11-16; see also Exod. 6:28–7:2).

Due to Moses' reluctance, his brother Aaron can speak in his place. God tells Moses to 'speak to' Aaron and 'put words in his mouth' and Aaron will be the 'mouth' of Moses. God points out that this models the way he deals with his prophets, where he speaks to his prophets and puts words in their mouths, so that when they speak, they are his 'mouth'.

Fourthly, Moses faithfully reports God's words. Moses obediently reports God's message accurately, without changing it, despite much opposition. In Moses' ministry, God repeatedly commands Moses to 'Go ... tell ...' or 'Go ... say ...' (for example, Exod. 3:16; 18; 4:12; 6:11; 8:1; 9:1; Deut. 5:30) and Moses obeys and faithfully reports God's message.

But, besides Moses, who else fits these criteria to become proclaimers of God's Word? In Deuteronomy 18, God promises, 'I will raise up for them a prophet like [Moses] ... I will put my words in his mouth, and he will tell them everything I command him' (Deut. 18:18). In other words, God promises to raise a future prophet in the model of Moses: he will be commissioned by God ('I will raise up...'), he will receive his words directly from God ('I will put my words in his mouth...') and he will faithfully report God's words ('he will tell them everything I command him'). Deuteronomy 18 does not mention any anointing by God's Spirit but perhaps implies it in the promise that the prophet will be 'raised up' by God 'like' Moses. As the Bible's storyline unfolds in the Old Testament, prophets follow in the footsteps of Moses, especially major figures such as Samuel, Elijah, Elisha, Isaiah, Jeremiah, Ezekiel and Amos.

In the New Testament, Jesus begins his earthly ministry by quoting this passage from Isaiah and then claiming that he has begun to fulfil it:

The Spirit of the Lord is on me, because he has anointed me to preach good news to the poor. He has sent me to proclaim freedom for the prisoners and recovery of sight for the blind, to release the oppressed, to proclaim the year of the Lord's favour (Luke 4:18-19).

In doing so, Jesus announces that he is commissioned by God ('He has sent me...') and anointed by God's Spirit ('The Spirit of the Lord is on me') to preach God's message. Jesus also implies that he has received his words from God (for he is commissioned and anointed) and he is about to faithfully proclaim it ('to preach good news to the poor ... to proclaim freedom for the prisoners ... to proclaim the year of the Lord's favour'). Among other things, Jesus claims to be the ultimate Prophet who fulfils the promise of Deuteronomy 18 – a prophet like Moses.

More importantly, Jesus is not merely like Moses, Jesus now replaces Moses as the chief Prophet, the chief proclaimer of God's Word. But it is even more than this. In John's Gospel, Jesus is called the Word because he himself is the message from God, namely, God becoming flesh and dwelling among us (John 1:14). To proclaim God's Word is the same as proclaiming Christ.

But at the end of Jesus' earthly ministry, just before he ascends to heaven, Jesus gives the same commission to his disciples or apostles:

'But you will receive power when the Holy Spirit comes on you; and you will be my witnesses in Jerusalem, and in all Judea and Samaria, and to the ends of the earth' (Acts 1:8).

As a result, the apostles now continue Jesus' earthly ministry; they are commissioned by Jesus and anointed by his Spirit to faithfully preach the message about Jesus. Notice how the commissioning and message are now transformed to be specifically Christocentric, that is, focussed upon Christ.

But we also discover that all Christians, not just the apostles, are to follow in the footsteps of Jesus. We are to continue Jesus' earthly ministry, part of which involves faithfully proclaiming God's Word.

Firstly, Christians have been commissioned by Jesus. For example, at the end of Matthew's Gospel, Jesus gives his disciples and all subsequent Christians a commission to 'go and make disciples of all nations ... teaching them to obey everything I have commanded you' (Matt. 28:19-20). This commission remains in effect until 'the very end of the age' (Matt. 28:20). In another example, Paul argues that we have been given 'the ministry of reconciliation' and are appointed as 'Christ's ambassadors, as though God were making his appeal through us' (2 Cor. 5:18-20).

Secondly, Christians have been anointed by the Spirit. At the day of Pentecost, when God pours out his Spirit upon the apostles, Peter claims that this marks the fulfilment of Joel's prophecy that in the last days all of God's people will have the Spirit and be empowered to prophesy (Acts 2:16-21).

Thirdly, Christians have received God's Word. In the New Testament, 'the Word of God' gradually came to refer more specifically to 'the gospel' – the news that Jesus Christ has come to be Lord and Saviour and all must repent and trust in Jesus. This 'Word' originally was Christ himself. But after Christ's ascension to heaven, 'the Word' referred to the gospel about Christ as proclaimed by the apostles and then as written (or inscripturated) in the texts of Scripture. All Christians have received this Word. For example, Peter encourages his readers by stating, 'For you have been born again ... through the living and enduring word of God. ...this is the word that was preached to you' (1 Pet. 1:23-25).

Fourthly, Christians are to faithfully report God's message. For example, Paul argues that God 'has committed to us the message of reconciliation' (2 Cor. 5:19). In another example, Paul exhorts Timothy, 'I give you this charge: Preach the Word...' (2 Tim. 4:2).

Therefore, in this survey of the Bible, we have found that the human proclaimers of God's Word have been commissioned by God and anointed by his Spirit. They have received their words from God and they faithfully proclaim the message that has been given to them. In the Old Testament, the model was Moses. But in the New Testament, Jesus not only becomes the model for his apostles and all Christians, but Jesus is also the message. As a Christian, to be a human proclaimer of God's Word is to be a faithful witness of the gospel of Jesus Christ.

3. The Spirit applies God's Word

We cannot overstate the importance of the Spirit in the preaching of God's Word. We have already examined, albeit too briefly, how the Spirit is necessary in preaching because he authors God's Word and empowers the preacher to proclaim God's Word. Without the Spirit, it is impossible for the preacher to proclaim God's Word. But the Spirit also has a role in the person who hears God's Word being preached.

What is this role?

A friend of mine once attended a class on preaching. As an exercise, the teacher took the class to a cemetery and asked them to preach to the graves. They preached but, of course, nothing happened (thankfully!). The exercise illustrated that if preaching relied only upon human words and communication skills, then our preaching cannot provoke anyone to faith, obedience and action. The teacher probably had in mind the vision from Ezekiel 37 where God commands Ezekiel to preach to a valley of dead bones. As Ezekiel preaches, God sends 'breath' (which is a Hebrew pun for 'Spirit') into the bones and they come alive. As part of the application of the vision, God announces, 'I will put my Spirit in you and you will live...' (Ezek. 37:14).

The Spirit is necessary in preaching because he enables the hearer to understand the preached Word. Notice Paul's argument to the Corinthian church:

> '[B]ut God has revealed it to us by his Spirit. The Spirit searches all things, even the deep things of God. For who among men knows the thoughts of a man except the man's spirit within him? In the same way no-one knows the thoughts of God except the Spirit of God. We have not received the spirit of the world but the Spirit who is from God, that we may understand what God has freely given us. This is what we speak, not in words taught us by human wisdom but in words taught by the Spirit, expressing

spiritual truths in spiritual words. The man without the Spirit does not accept the things that come from the Spirit of God, for they are foolishness to him, and he cannot understand them, because they are spiritually discerned' (1 Cor. 2:10-14).

A person with the Spirit, who has experienced the regenerating and illuminating work of the Spirit, can understand the preached Word, of which the Spirit is the original author. But a person without the Spirit lacks the ability to recognise the wisdom of God's words.

The Spirit is also necessary because he guides people to the truth, moving the hearer of God's Word to faith, obedience and action. In John 14–16, Jesus promises to send the Spirit who will teach the disciples and remind them of Jesus' teachings (14:26); testify to Jesus (15:26-27); convict the world regarding sin, righteousness and judgement (16:8-11); guide them to truth (16:13); and glorify Jesus (16:14). This promise was fulfilled by the Spirit's work in guiding the apostles when they preached the gospel and wrote the New Testament. But it is also being fulfilled by the Spirit's ongoing work, as he continues to guide people today. The Spirit uses the teachings and testimonies of Jesus, as inscripturated in the Scriptures, and proclaimed through the preaching of God's Word, to testify to and glorify Christ, guide people to the truth and convict them regarding sin, righteousness and judgement.

Therefore, in this survey of the Bible, we have seen that the Spirit applies God's Word in the life of the hearer. The Spirit enables the hearer to understand what has been preached and then moves the hearer to respond in faith, obedience and action.

We began with a suggested definition: Preaching is a joint activity between God and the preacher – God speaking his Word, through the human proclamation of God's Word, which the Spirit applies to the hearer. This definition was supported by our survey through the Bible's storyline. We have seen that preaching is a joint activity that involves a partnership between God and the human preacher. God speaks and the preacher faithfully proclaims God's Word. But we can also note that preaching is a Trinitarian activity, in which God speaks his Word, this Word is the gospel about Jesus Christ, and the Spirit is the one who authors God's Word, empowers the preacher to preach God's Word and applies God's Word to the hearer.

2.

THE SPEAKER AS A PERSON

STUART COULTON

When Augustine of Canterbury came to evangelise England he met with the leaders of what remained of the original church in Britain. These folk had been pushed by invading armies back into what is today Wales. It was 603 AD, and the Welsh delegation was unsure whether to listen to Augustine's demands that they change the date at which they celebrated Easter. They consulted an elderly hermit for wisdom, asking him whether they ought to do Augustine's bidding.

'Yes,' said the hermit, 'if he is a man of God'.
    'And how shall we know that?'
    'If this Augustine is gentle and lowly in heart, we may believe that he ... bears the yoke of Christ .... but if he is harsh and arrogant, it is plain he is not from God ...'
    'And how shall we tell which he is?'
    'Why ... if he rises to greet you, you will know that he is a servant of Christ.'
    They met with Augustine. He remained seated and did not show them Christian respect. It was 1188 before the breach was finally healed![1]

This account is a useful reminder that ministry is more than strategy and preaching more than giftedness. The character

---

[1] Bruce, *The Spreading Flame*, Eerdmans, 1958. Reprinted 1995, p 400.

of the man or woman who speaks from God's Word cannot be separated from the message they proclaim.

When Paul reflected upon his ministry in Thessalonica he was able to write,

'We loved you so much that we were delighted to share not only the gospel of God but our lives as well' (1 Thess. 2:8).

Paul did not proclaim the gospel in isolation from who he was, the manner of man Christ had made him. He was able to call the Thessalonians as witnesses to the blameless way he lived among them (1 Thess. 2:10). The truth of his message was backed by the integrity of his life.

What we do cannot be separated from who we are. If the gospel transforms the whole person then the man or woman who speaks that Word does matter. There are five characteristics I have chosen, which mark anyone who would teach God's Word.

1. Someone who is walking with God

The speaker ought firstly to know God intimately. While this may seem obvious, true knowledge of God is not simply formal, objective knowledge. It is all-consuming, passionate and life changing. Henri Nouwen said that the leaders of the church in the twenty-first century '...cannot simply be persons who have well-informed opinions about the burning issues of our time. Their leadership must be rooted in the permanent, intimate relationship with the incarnate Word, Jesus ...'[2]

It is a terrible error to imagine that what God does *through* us is divorced from what he does *in* us. How can we prepare Bible talks, preach in churches and lead Bible studies that will assist people to develop healthy, intimate relationships with God, without seeking that same intimate walk with Jesus for ourselves?

Frederick Buechner says of the preacher:

'Poor, bare, forked animal in his cassock with his heart in his mouth if not yet his foot. What can he say? ...He is called

---

[2] H. Nouwen, *In the Name of Jesus*, Darton, Longman & Todd, 1989, p 31.

not to be an actor, a magician, in the pulpit. He is called to be himself.'[3]

In other words we must speak truth that we have experienced for ourselves. The alternative is hypocrisy. In many areas of life dispassionate and detached objectivity is highly prized. However, in matters of the heart – relationships with wives and husbands, children and friends and especially with God – objective truth must always transform us. Jesus spoke of being 'born again' (John 3:3) and the truth setting us free (John 8:32), whilst Paul wrote of being 'transformed by the renewing of your mind' (Rom. 12:1-2). If the truth we preach is not firstly doing its work in us then we are hypocritical to proclaim that truth to others. The speaker must know God to speak with integrity about God.

Martyn Lloyd-Jones defined preaching as 'logic on fire'.[4] This is so much more than technique – learning the right words and gestures to communicate conviction. It is a matter of the mind and heart being gripped by who God is and all that he has done – God's glory. While we cannot and should not be seeking a continual emotional 'high', we ought not to rest content with a walk with God that is cold and formal. It is essential that we should have right doctrine concerning Jesus, but equally important that we should be 'in love' with Jesus! (Luke 10:27)

The teacher of God's Word must be willing to give care and attention to developing an intimate walk with God. This will engage him/her in the work of careful and systematic study of the Bible, in the context of prayer, fellowship and reflection upon what God is doing in their life. More will be said about some of these points later, but firstly a few comments on the latter two.

It is astonishingly easy to regularly teach the Bible to a congregation or a Bible study group without making yourself accountable to the fellowship of that group of people.

---

[3] F. Buechner, *Telling the Truth,* Harper, 1977, p 40.
[4] M. Lloyd-Jones, *Preaching and Preachers*, Hodder & Stoughton, London, 1981, p 97.

The 'role' of teacher sets us apart and ever so subtly we begin to imagine that because we teach the Bible to them, they have nothing to teach us. It requires particular attention to and prayer for humility if we are to balance the authority we exercise in teaching with our need for accountability to the fellowship of God's people.

In the same way, we must train ourselves to observe what God is doing in our lives. Keeping a journal where we can reflect on what the Scriptures are teaching us, record the lessons learnt from our involvement with people, discipline ourselves to be attentive to God's Holy Spirit as he speaks to us through the Word and bears his fruit in us – in this way we give ourselves time and opportunity to engage in the 'cure' of our own souls (to take an ancient phrase given modern application by Eugene Peterson[5]) in order to be engaged in the cure of others.

2. *Someone who is labouring in prayer*

The second activity is prayer. Thousands of words have been written about the need for Christian people to pray. Still, somehow, in the rush of work and children, marriage and mortgages, sermon preparation and pastoral care – have you ever found yourself standing to preach and realised that the one thing missing has been a heartfelt prayerfulness for you, your preparation and for those about to listen? It can easily happen if we are not committed to the work of prayer.

So how can this happen, given the things that we believe about prayer? Eugene Peterson suggests that pastoral work itself erodes prayer. The expectations placed upon us, by ourselves as much as those to whom we minister, crowd out prayer. Prayer is too often seen as the luxury item in a hectic schedule. Unconsciously we substitute our activity for our prayers. As Ben Patterson writes: 'Many of us feel we have too much to *do* to have time to pray.... At bottom we don't believe we are really *doing* anything when we pray – other than pray, that is'.[6]

---

[5] E. Peterson, *The Contemplative Pastor*, Eerdmans, 1989.
[6] *Leadership* Winter 1995.

Yet how can we imagine that we can walk with God or preach God's Word without prayer? Prayer was central to Jesus' life and ministry (Mark 1:35; 6:46; 14:32ff); Paul asked for prayer for his ministry (Col. 4:3-4) and the richness of his prayer-life is woven throughout the text of his letters. Paul's friend Epaphras 'worked hard in prayer' for the Colossian Christians (Col 4:12-13). Perhaps we do not see prayer as our serious work – as much a part of preparing a talk as the work of exegesis and application.

Perhaps we need a good dose of discipline! Relationships work best when we are focused on them, self-controlled and intentional. Do you demand of yourself that you pray? Have you planned how you might best pray and set in place habits that will enable you to pray? The pattern I seek for myself is to build the prayers of Paul into my own prayers for people (*A Call to Spiritual Reformation* by Don Carson is a great help in this); to keep learning how to turn the Psalms into my own prayers; and to walk while I intercede (keeps the soul fit as well as the body – and the dog!). Find a pattern and work at it until good habits form.

A strong doctrine of God's sovereignty, the present activity of the Holy Spirit and a sense of our own neediness is required if we are to practise our own theology of prayer. Whilst it is important to invest in learning the craft of sermon preparation and leading Bible studies, the danger is that we imagine our skill level will determine the effectiveness of our work. It is God who brings people to repentance and faith. If our teaching is not anointed by the Holy Spirit and applied by him to our listeners, then they may well have heard a fine piece of rhetoric, but they have not engaged with the living God! So pray!

3. Someone who is meditating on God's Word
Martin Luther said that prayer, meditation and temptation make the theologian. Having spoken of prayer, let's now turn to meditation on God's Word. The one who speaks from God's Word must be willing to live under the authority of that Word. This requires firstly a willingness to read and meditate upon the Word. Robert Murray M'Cheyne, a nineteenth century Scottish pastor, encouraged systematic and *wide* reading of

the Bible – breadth as well as depth, together with a prayerful meditation upon that Word. M'Cheyne's own programme for Bible reading is one way to achieve this end. It will take you in one year through the New Testament and Psalms twice and the Old Testament once (or in two years if you choose to halve the readings and use Don Carson's excellent *For the Love of God* as a devotional commentary).

Henri Nouwen warned that, 'Reading the Scriptures is not as easy as it seems since in our academic world we tend to make anything and everything we read subject to analysis and discussion'.[7]

There is nothing wrong with that of course, but if that is all we do then we run the risk of placing ourselves over the Word and not under it. We risk placing God's Word at arm's length and reducing it down to a textbook. Nouwen suggests the need for silence in our reading of God's Word to allow for meditation. Clearing our minds and our lives of clamour for a period of time so that we might focus upon God's Word, reflect prayerfully upon it and allow God's Spirit to do his work in us through that Word. In our increasingly businesslike model for ministry this may not sit comfortably – but we impoverish ourselves if we do not make space and slow ourselves down for reflective study of the Bible.

Secondly, as someone speaking from and living under God's Word, there must be a willingness to act upon that Word. Jesus warns against the sin of hypocrisy in religious leaders (Matt. 23). There is much truth in Dietrich Bonhoeffer's words that 'All along the line we are trying to evade the obligation of single-minded literal obedience'.[8] Those who would teach God's Word must be uncompromising in their commitment to obey that Word. Charles Spurgeon wrote that 'The life of the preacher should be a magnet to draw men to Christ...'[9]

Giftedness is important in a speaker. Consistent holiness is essential. Yet how easy it is to reverse them! On the one hand we have been too busy to spend time in meditative study of God's Word, and our relationships within the family are,

---

[7] H. Nouwen, *Reaching Out,* Fount, 1975, p 103.

[8] D. Bonhoeffer, *The Cost of Discipleship*, SCM Press, 1959, p 71.

[9] C. H. Spurgeon, *Lectures to My Students*, 'Lecture I'.

frankly, a bit of a mess. On the other hand the talk has to be given; the Bible study has to be led. What do we do? Most of us still get up to speak. Now from time to time that may not be ideal but it is realistic. However, when we 'get away with it' once or twice we start imagining that we don't need to live under the Word in order to teach it; that we can honour God by faithfully teaching others how to live, even though we are not living it for ourselves. This gap between the talk and the walk can become fixed in us.

Paul's command to Timothy was that he 'set an example for the believers in speech, in life, in love, in faith and in purity' (1 Tim. 4:12), devoting himself to the teaching of Scripture (13). In Paul's mind the link is clear – Timothy's teaching was to be reflected in a consistent life of obedience. Those who teach God's Word would do well to remember the words of Robert Murray M'Cheyne that 'The greatest need of my people is my personal holiness'.

If we commit ourselves to live with repentance under the authority of the Word we teach then we will seek out ways to hide God's Word in our hearts 'that I might not sin against you' (Ps. 119:11). Systematic study of the Bible; wide reading of the Bible; turning the Bible into prayer (another M'Cheyne phrase); using a journal to reflect on what the Lord is doing in your life – these are but a few ways we will seek integrity of lifestyle to stand alongside our teaching of God's Word.

4. Someone who enjoys loving people

Paul's letter to the Thessalonian church provides a remarkable insight into the way he viewed those to whom he ministered. Paul tells the church they are his 'glory and joy' (1 Thess. 2:19-20), describing how he 'loved you so much that we were delighted to share with you not only the gospel of God but our lives as well' (1 Thess. 2:8). It is important that those who teach should also be lovingly involved in the lives of the people they serve.

Someone who engages in any form of itinerant teaching (and almost everyone who teaches will do so at one time or another) will realise how difficult it is to form any kind of connection with the people you teach. That is a necessary part of itinerant ministry; however, most of us conduct our teaching ministry within a settled pastoral setting. The pastor of a church who teaches Sunday by Sunday, the elder who preaches once a month or the home group leader who prepares weekly Bible studies – all have a pastoral bond with those they teach.

The danger is that we develop an 'itinerant' mindset. We decide to leave to others (consciously or not) the pastoral engagement, the involvement in the messiness of people's lives. Our task, we argue, is to teach. We are practising job specialization; letting others do the work of pastoral care. In doing so we fail to recognise that while people accept that a visiting speaker will be emotionally remote from those he/she teaches, most people do not expect that kind of disengagement from those who regularly teach God's Word to them.

Teaching God's Word is a relational act. A part of our authority comes from the integrity of the relationship we have with those we teach. The way we apply the passage we are preaching will be shaped by the pastoral relationship we have with our people. Our understanding of their needs and their respect for us as their pastor/Bible study leader is built upon our involvement in the at times muddled and often painful details of their life. It is too often an excuse to argue that our people cannot have both our head and our feet. The reality is they need and deserve both!

If we are not lovingly involved in the lives of the people we teach, if we cannot say (with Paul) that we love them enough to share not only the Word with them but a part of ourselves, then we must pause to consider, why not?

Someone who is living in the furnace
Martin Luther said that the test of the pastor is this:

'Does he know of death and the Devil?
Or is it all sweetness and light?'

By nature we do all we can to spare ourselves from pain and suffering, doubt and dark times. Nonetheless, it is often through these times that our faith is strengthened as we live the reality of what we believe and experience the truth of what we teach. The teacher's place is not in the audience (meaning the study or office) watching the action and making judicious remarks to the actors about how they might improve their performance.

Clearly Paul's faith had been forged in the context of suffering (2 Cor. 4). He knew what it meant to be tested, to suffer for the gospel. He asked of others only what he had been willing to endure himself (2 Tim. 1:8; 3:10-14). Those who would teach must have a faith that has been 'lived in'. The experience of suffering in the spiritual battle that rages is one that not only refines our faith. It also gives us a capacity for understanding the sufferings of others as they seek to work out what it means to believe in a world that groans 'as in the pains of childbirth' (Rom. 8:22).

Years ago, working as a lawyer, my response to any client whose suffering overflowed into my office was to offer to make them a cup of tea – and wait till they felt better. I quickly learnt that this approach did not translate well into ministry! Paul described himself as a father who comforts his children and as a mother who cared for her little children (1 Thess. 2:1-12).

So don't despise (or avoid) hospitals and crematoriums. Immerse yourself in the traumas of redundancies and divorces. Engage with people's hopes and disappointments. While these arenas may not be where suffering is directly linked to the persecutions and struggles that Paul spoke of, it is often in these contexts that people are seeking to live out their faith, deal with their doubts and witness to Christ. The study may well be an attractive place for us – a world where we feel in control and one which gives us a great sense of satisfaction – however, we also belong in the world of the people we teach. We may well feel a lot less in control, it can be costly in terms of our time and energy. But unless we live with a foot in each, we cannot exegete both text and people.

'Not many of you should presume to be teachers, my brothers, because you know that we who teach will be judged more strictly' (James 3:1). James' words should cause us to pause and reflect before we take on the great task of teaching. It is in very few activities that *who we are* is as important as *what we do*. Teaching God's Word is one such activity.

3.

PRAYER AND PREPARATION

DUDLEY FOORD

Prayer is indispensable

The process of sermon preparation from beginning to end has been described by an African-American preacher as 'First, I reads myself full, next I thinks myself clear, next I prays myself hot, and then I lets go!'

While this warm, humorous statement is full of valuable insights, it leaves the impression that prayer is to be left to the very end of the preparation process. However, it is vital to include prayer at all phases of the preparation; the selection of the Biblical passage; the background reading; the textual study; the thinking; the development of an outline/structure; the choice of words; the use of illustration and the application to the hearers.

We begin with prayer and continue not only in an attitude of prayer but by frequently pausing and crying out to God in prayer for wisdom, understanding and the illumination of the Holy Spirit from beginning to end. In addition, after preaching, we continue to pray that Satan will not pluck the Word from people's hearts and minds; but that the Word proclaimed will accomplish the task of turning people to Christ as Lord and causing godly and holy living.

Why is prayer so essential in the preparation process?
In the four Gospels there are seventeen examples of Christ at prayer. Clearly he saw prayer as crucial. It is notable that in Christ's teaching on prayer, he emphasised persistence and perseverance in prayer. 'Men ought always to pray and not give up' (Luke 18:1), and that God's people should 'Cry out to him day and night' (Luke 18:7).

The churches in the Acts of the Apostles seemed to be saturated in prayer. Paul and the other apostles show us how God invites us to be his co-workers in the great enterprise of proclaiming God's Word. We are totally dependent upon God for the results that follow. Paul in his letters in the New Testament is a good model for us. He frequently urges his readers to 'pray for us that the message of the Lord may spread rapidly...' (2 Thess. 3:1). He also urges us to pray for all people that they may be saved (1 Tim. 2:3-4). Again he writes '...as you help us by your prayers. Then many will give thanks ... for the gracious favour granted us in answer to the prayers of many' (2 Cor. 1:11). There is a close connection between intercessory prayer and God powerfully acting.

Taken together, the intercessory prayers in Paul's letters are an impressive model of his unfailing reliance on the importance of prayer, and this shaped his understanding of the gospel and the exercise of his preaching ministry.

Spurgeon urged preachers, 'Be much with God in holy dialogue, letting him speak to you by his word while you speak back to him by your prayers'.[1] Is it possible that so much preaching seems so powerless because we have paid too little attention to prayer and to the promises of Christ to empower us by his Spirit as we prepare and then preach?

Recognition of the importance of prayer in sermon preparation could be responded to by a cold sense of duty in a mechanical, brief, perfunctory prayer as one commences the arduous task of preparation. I sadly fell into that error early in my preaching ministry. My preparation consisted entirely in expositional work of the biblical text. Certainly I took that aspect of preparation very seriously, but prayer

---

[1] C. H. Spurgeon, *An All-round Ministry*, 1960, p 340.

was absent. It was straight mental work, reading, reflecting and writing.

But now, interspersing this, there is constant and frequent lifting of my heart in prayer. Crying out to God, I pour out my heart to him for wisdom, insight and for the illumination of his Spirit in rightly grasping the text, the structuring of a sermon, and the right application to the hearers.

The truths of the Bible and the mode in which they must be grasped far surpass our human powers. Thus prayer and the godly life of the one preparing a Bible talk stand at the heart of the task of interpretation and sermon preparation. Ignoring this will make a significant difference in the process of preparation and the sermon itself. It has been said, 'Work without prayer is atheism and prayer without work is presumption'.[2]

The preacher – growing in humility and godliness through prayer

Humility is one of the greatest virtues in the Bible, as pride is one of the greatest sins. God 'resists the proud, but gives grace to the humble' (James 4:6). Today's culture has no place for humility; it is for weaklings and losers. Winners are those who constantly exude self-confidence and superiority. But in sharp contrast, the godly, humble man listens to and obeys God's Word. 'For this is what the high and lofty One says – he who lives forever, whose name is holy: "I live in a high and holy place, but also with him who is contrite and lowly in spirit..."' (Isa. 57:15).

Moreover, the preacher is to train himself to be godly (1 Tim. 4:7). This injunction to grow in godliness can only be achieved by regular, unremitting, disciplined meditation on the Bible and prayer. Regular time alone with the Father is a weak point with many of us. The excitement of ministry that puts us 'out the front' has an attraction for us that the calm and the quiet of being alone with our Heavenly Father do not possess. Certainly ministry 'out the front' is important but it carries large dangers. Ministry makes something of us.

---

[2] R. W. Dale, *Lectures in Preaching*, 1900, p 91.

Through it we can acquire prestige, which appeals to us more than being alone with God, because in the presence of God we are nothing and our human nature finds that irksome. Soon it is possible to lose real spiritual freshness and we allow by osmosis the level and mindset of our culture to take over. In this state the most glorious and soul-stirring realities are soon held as mere propositions and are preached as such. This is a great disaster for the preacher and soon complacency and self-satisfaction dominate.

We will also find that the real danger is not so much our conscious weaknesses but our fancied strengths. At the points where we know we are vulnerable we are most careful. In the case of our strong points we are most often off our guard and Satan achieves an easy conquest. This will quickly impact and spoil our preaching and public speaking. We need to take to heart Jesus' words that 'without me you can do nothing' (John 15:5). The preacher needs to exhibit at all times humility, courage, genuine sincerity and earnestness together with the gentleness of Christ. We are constantly to humble ourselves under the hand of Almighty God (1 Pet. 5:6) growing in Christ-likeness and in prayer.

The sermon – truth on fire in the pulpit!

A preacher may desire and prepare well to preach an expository sermon, but in the pulpit adopt a lecture-style teaching approach. Furthermore, the sermon lacks apt and interesting illustrations and also fails to make appropriate application of the Word of God to the mind and heart of the hearers. Preaching can be doctrinally and biblically accurate but dull, cold, boring and spiritually lifeless. Such preachers conjure up the image of somebody carefully fingering and explaining each bone of a skeleton. Effective preachers enflesh the skeleton so that it comes to life as a dynamic entity, powerfully gripping the minds of the hearers, addressing the conscience and moving the will to act, decide, choose and obey God's word.

The truths of the Bible are not bare propositional statements, but powerful influences. We are to feel the force of these truths and become so familiar with them that they fill our minds and hearts and move our emotions. When doctrines are preached with feeling, warmth and passion they will move people. It would be good to see congregations thrilled and excited by the Word of God. Such emotion is exhilarating, infectious and God-honouring.

The Psalmist surely expressed such a principle when he wrote, 'my heart grew hot within me, and as I meditated, the fire burned; then I spoke with my tongue' (Ps. 39:3). God's message within us should be like a burning fire as with Jeremiah, 'His word is in my heart like a fire, a fire shut up in my bones. I am weary of holding it in; indeed, I cannot' (Jer. 20:9). It must be our settled practice to give ourselves to prayer as we prepare so that God will cause his Word to burn within us; and that our hearts will experience the explosive power of God's living and powerful Word. Then surely, truth will be on fire in the pulpit.

The preparation process and prayer
The preparation of a Bible talk or sermon is a multi-faceted task, enormously exacting and demanding, requiring many hours of painstaking hard work and study. We certainly need to utilise all the books and tools available to us, but since the sermon is focused on the great eternal spiritual truths of God's Word, it is important to recognize that human study and activity alone is not sufficient. At all points in the preparation process it is crucial that we do it in a prayerful attitude, intermingling human study with frequent, fervent prayer. This is a difficult aspect of preparation and it is feared we may be deficient at this point.

I have identified eight stages in the preparation process:

1. Selection of biblical text
This may be your choice or you are allocated part of a series. If the responsibility rests on you to plan the preaching programme, then considerable thought, reflection, consultation and prayer will be necessary. To provide a balanced biblical diet for a congregation is a weighty matter requiring lots of work and constant prayer.

2. Meditation on the biblical text
Read the relevant section of the Bible and reread it again and again. Immerse and saturate yourself in it. Allow it to soak into

35

you. Go on wrestling with what the passage is all about; the longer this period the better. Some may have several weeks before they are scheduled to preach, others may have a weekly obligation. Nothing must replace your own personal encounter with the biblical text.

It is a very helpful pattern to spend, say, thirty minutes each day before you preach, meditating and reflecting on the passage. Each day crying out to God in prayer, as you meditate on the text, so that the 'eyes of your heart may be enlightened...' (Eph. 1:18). You will discover that this act of daily meditation on God's Word will impact your life, changing you – your attitude, your behaviour. A sermon prepared in this way will carry an authentic, realistic quality that readily connects with the hearer.

3. Study the biblical text – engage in wider reading
Work hard on the text. Address questions to it:

(i) What does it say (to the original readers)?
(ii) What does it mean?
(iii) How does it apply to us today?

You are searching for the contemporary meaning and bridging from the world of the Bible to today's world. Keep praying for the Spirit of God to show you how.

4. Look for the big idea – the main theme of the biblical text
A sermon differs from the verse-by-verse pattern of a lecture style Bible study. Instead we look for the dominant theme. We search out one main idea that encapsulates one major message. We then express that one major point in a short crystal clear, pregnant phrase. This is a difficult task and we need to call on God for illumination and help.

5. Develop a structure – arrange your material – choice of words
Our overriding purpose is to allow the passage we are expounding to speak for itself. We desire God's Word to be clearly heard. No sermon is strong without a structure. We want to open up the text like a rose bud opening up and displaying its hidden beauty. Avoid abstract nouns and too many conceptual

statements. Always choose words that are concrete, vivid and clear. Prayer is indispensable in this process.

6. Use of illustrations, introduction and conclusion
See Chapters 6 and 8 in this book.

7. Write out the sermon
See all relevant chapters in this book.

8. Pray over this sermon
We have been active at all points in this complex task; a dual combination of human study and much prayer. Arrow-like prayers such as Nehemiah's – quick, brief requests to God – and prayers searching our own hearts and motives. But now we need to give further time to calling on God to possess our minds and hearts with his Word and causing this Word to burn in our inner beings.

A final reflection
Well might we exclaim, 'Who is sufficient for these things? The task is beyond me; it is enormously taxing and demanding!'

'[God] has made us competent as ministers of a new covenant' (2 Cor. 3:6). The whole message of 2 Corinthians is of God's power in our weaknesses. We must live constantly under the authority of God's Word. 'This is the one I esteem: he who is humble and contrite in spirit, and trembles at my word' (Isa. 66:2).

The Word of God must be our teacher not we its critics. Play to the audience of one – the Lord Christ. We preach and speak in the awesome presence of the Living God. He sees and hears all. Preach with one person and one object in mind – the greatest glory of Jesus Christ our Lord.

SECTION 2

PREPARING YOUR MATERIAL

4.

INTERPRETING GOD'S WORD

LEIGH TREVASKIS

The long distance relationship is a relationship of the *word*. A line of words from a girlfriend's pen can cause more emotional turmoil than a line spoken by her in your presence. The problem with love letters is that they go unaccompanied by their author and they are interpreted by a brain lying in a love-induced stupor. Well, that was how it was for me. Most of us would prefer meeting our beloved author face to face rather than in her *words*. This applies to our relationship with God too. He likewise speaks to us in written *words* rather than face to face. It is true, God revealed himself fully to us in the person of Jesus – *the* Word (John 1:1-18). However, *the* Word of God's revelation is remembered by interpreting all the words written about him. God meets us clothed in literature.

As for the readily misinterpreted love letter, the Bible's human authors are absent and can't help us interpret. Moreover, the mists of time, culture, and sin have fiddled with the sights of our interpretative aim. The perfect interpretation remains a future hope for when we will see Christ 'face to face' (1 Cor. 13:12). So how should we approach the task of interpreting these words in the meantime?

Well, the Bible's purpose indicates that a correct interpretation is possible. Whereas the love letter's purpose is to conform its *intended* interpreter to the author's likeness for them, the Bible seeks to conform its *intended* interpreter to Christ's likeness, so that they will be equipped for service in Christ's church (2 Tim. 3:17). Since the Bible intends to be understood by anyone united with Christ, this chapter looks at the work of biblical interpretation from the perspective of union with Christ – union with the one who is known to us in words.

Interpreting your new identity 'in Christ'

Your union with Christ makes you a Bible interpreter. Biblical interpretation is the oxygen pipe that allows your new identity 'in Christ' to breathe and become embodied in your daily living. 'In Christ' is Paul's shorthand reference to this union (1 Cor. 1:5; Eph. 1:6-7; 1 Thess. 4:14, 16). It refers to being counted as righteous and holy as you live, by faith, under Christ's representative headship (Gal. 2:20), rather than Adam's deathly one (Rom. 5:19). You now bear Christ's righteousness rather than Adam's guilt.

It works like this. Christ became a human (Phil. 2:5-11) so that he could be crucified *for* you (2 Cor. 5:15, 21) and raised to life *for* you (Rom. 4:25). This means that *by faith* you died *with* Christ to sin's slavery (Rom. 6:6-7) and were resurrected *with* him to 'walk a new life' of obedience to the Father (Rom. 6:4, 10-11). This death and resurrection is as real as Christ's because the Spirit's indwelling bonds you to him leaving 'no gulf in time or space' (1 Cor. 12:13. cf. 6:17, 19; Rom. 8:9-11).[1] You really are a new creation 'in Christ' (2 Cor. 5:17).

It is your union with Christ that motivates obedient living (e.g. 1 Cor. 6:12-20; Eph. 4:20-32. cf. 2:1-10). You were redeemed *from* the slavery of sin *for* conformity to your new identity 'in Christ' (Col. 3:1-10). To know how to be conformed to your new righteous and holy identity requires your interpretation of the words about Christ. Understandably, when this aspect of the life of faith is neglected '...*the remembered Christ becomes an imagined Christ, shaped by the religiosity and the unconscious*

---

[1] John Calvin, *Institutes of the Christian Religion*, Ed. J. T. McNeill. Trans. F.L. Battles. 2 Vols. Westminster, Philadelphia, 1960 III. i. 1.

desires of his worshipers.[2] A 'Christ' who bears a remarkable resemblance to your 'old man'! That's the point. When you neglect interpretation, you're left to live like your 'old man' – a dead man whom God no longer acknowledges (Eph. 4:20-32; Col. 3:9-10) – instead of your new man 'in Christ' (Gal. 3:27). So the work of interpretation is not just for the theologically trained Christian, but for anybody who has been united with God's Son and raised to live a new life. God's Spirit moulds and shapes us through his rightly understood Word.

Your new status as an interpreter

Distance is the problem of the love letter; mental (that is, love stupefied) and geographical distance. Distance is the problem of biblical interpretation too. *Historical* and *moral* distance.[3] *Historical,* because the human authors, along with their language and life-setting, are dead. *Moral,* because our sinfulness can prevent us from understanding the text correctly. However, both of these are potentially overcome for the interpreter united with Christ.

The historical distance overcome: God accompanies his words

I said that the problem with love letters is that they go un-accompanied by their authors. The author can't correct any wrong-headed meanings that the interpreter might bring to the letter (for example, 'I met a really funny bloke called Damien on Church Camp' could easily be misinterpreted to mean 'I'm torn between choosing between you and a bloke called Damien, whom I met on Church Camp.'). In contrast, God the Spirit, who was instrumental in the authorship of the Bible's words (2 Tim. 3:16-17; Acts 4:25; 28:25; Heb. 3:7; 10:15; 2 Pet. 1:21), also accompanies these words to help the interpreter understand and respond.

An appreciation of how the Father, Son and Spirit work together in revelation makes it easier to understand the Spirit's role in interpretation. The Father is the author of truth,

---

[2] J. D, Smart, *The Strange Silence of the Bible in the Church*, SCM Press, London, 1970, p 25.

[3] The phrase is from Kevin J, Vanhoozer, *Is There a Meaning in this Text?* Zondervan, Grand Rapids, Michigan, 1998 p 430.

uttering words in the past and finally speaking through the Son (Heb. 1:1-2). The Son is the Word of revelation – the text – who makes the Father known (John 1:18). The Spirit's role is to witness to and bring about the *consequence* of the Word's purpose (1 John 5:7). For example, God uses his Word to *save* you (James 1:18) – a mission accomplished in co-operation with the Spirit (Titus 3:5); God's Word makes you *holy* (John 17:17-19; Acts 20:32; Eph. 5:26) – by the sanctifying work of the Spirit (2 Thess. 2:13; 1 Pet 1:3) and God's Word *enlightens* your mind (Ps. 119:105; 2 Tim. 3:16) – but not without the agency of the Spirit either (John 14:26; 16:13; 1 Cor. 2:10-15). So the Spirit is the one who enables understanding and response to the meaning of God's Word (John 16:12-15). He ministers God's Word (Christ) to the Bible's readers. That's why the Bible can be called 'living and active' (Heb. 4:12) and the 'sword of the Spirit' (Eph. 6:17).

The Spirit doesn't add meaning to the Bible in the process of interpretation. He only witnesses to the truth (John 16:13) by bringing you to the senses of your 'new man' in Christ, reforming your sin-corrupted mind so that you can gain true knowledge of God (1 Cor. 2:9-16). He enables you to be taught about all things (1 John 2:20, 27) so that you may know God better (Eph. 1:17) and understand the mysteries of Christ (Eph. 3:5). Not since Moses have human beings had such access to God's truth (2 Cor. 3:12-4:6). Pray that God's Spirit would be active in your life, helping you to respond in repentance to the truths that you come across in Scripture (Eph. 1:17-19; 3:14-19). He is the one who works to conform you to Christ's image (Acts 2:33; Rom. 8:26; John 16:12-16).

The moral distance is overcome: interpreting from the perspective of your new man
Unbelievers interpret the Bible blindly (1 Cor. 2:14; 2 Cor. 4:3-4). They are dead in their sin (Eph. 2:1) and interpret the work of Christ as foolishness (1 Cor. 1:18). Not so for interpreters united with Christ. They have been raised to life (Eph. 2:5-6) and given the 'mind of Christ' (1 Cor. 2:15-16)[4] and 'the light

---

[4] That is, the believer *can* comprehend the wisdom of Christ crucified.

of the knowledge of the glory of God *in the face of Christ* (2 Cor. 4:6). Understanding what God intended in Scripture is now a real possibility for them. 'Reflect on what I am saying, for the Lord will give you insight into all this' (2 Tim. 2:7).

Nevertheless, your interpretative ability has, like the rest of you, been corrupted by sin. We still wait for the time of free-dom from sin's corruption (Rom. 8:18-25; 2 Cor. 4:4-5). In the meantime, heed God's command to kill off your 'old man's' ways (Col. 3:5) and become what you already are 'in Christ' (Col. 3:4; 1 John 3:2-3). Christ makes himself known to those who comply with his Father's will for them (John 14:21). Moreover, slothfulness in this task threatens your ability to interpret the Bible (1 Cor. 3:1-3), which will in turn impinge on your, and your church's, growth in Christ-likeness (Eph. 4:11-16). So, like Paul, desire to become like Christ in his death and resurrection (Phil. 3:10-11) so that you no longer employ your 'old man's' interpretative methods that suppressed and distorted the truth (Rom. 1:18; 2 Cor. 4:2; Eph. 4:17-19). A sentence like, 'Sell your possessions and give to the poor (Luke 12:33)' can sometimes set us scrambling for an interpretation that ensures that we don't need to sell a thing! That's the 'old man's' interpretative method that needs to be avoided. Instead, we are to humble ourselves under God's Word and be open to the possibility that we may have to change.

Serving God as the author of human literature
Recognition that you have been redeemed as an interpreter means that you have been redeemed from slavery to sin for the service of God.[5] With regards to biblical interpretation you're required to serve God as the Bible's author. God has declared that his Word will always achieve what he, as the author, desires (Isa. 55:11). The incarnation of his Son proves this. God the Son incarnate was the exact representation of the Father, called 'God with us' (Matt. 1:23). All of God's fullness dwelt in his body (Col. 1:19) and his face reflected the knowledge and

---

[5] If space had permitted something would also have been said about the diversity of interpretations within the redeemed community of the church. For those interested see Vanhoozer, *Is There a Meaning?* p 416-431.

the glory of God (2 Cor. 4:6). God can communicate himself meaningfully to us!

Now your respect for God as author must go further than merely believing that truth can be found in Scripture. A respect for the way in which God has used literature is also necessary. He has used many different literary types, at different times in history, to communicate with us.[6] Imagine if I were to read *The Lion, the Witch and the Wardrobe* as history. Not only might I develop a pathological habit of walking into the back of my uncle's wardrobe, but I would have disrespectfully ignored C. S. Lewis' decision to use allegory. In line with this, to begin interpreting all the Bible's literary types according to one set of rules (for example, historically) would assault God's message with your own enforced rules for reading; rules that God never intended to be used. True respect for God's authorship should lead you to ask the following questions of the text:[7]

1. What is the text's straightforward meaning?

This does not mean that all texts should be read literally, but that you should follow the text's own rules for reading. 'Peter, an apostle of Jesus Christ, To God's elect...' invites you to read 1 Peter as a letter. 'In the thirtieth year, in the fourth month on the fifth day, while I was among the exiles...' invites you to take the historical content of the book of Ezekiel into account. Some literary types are easier to read than others. The pastoral letters are closer to the literature we are used to reading in our culture than, say, apocalyptic (for example, Dan. 7–12 and Revelation). This means that you will have to work harder at interpreting the latter. You may need to refer to a good commentary that can guide your understanding of apocalyptic literature's sometimes confusing imagery.

2. What did the text mean to its original readers?

After taking into account the text's natural reading, you need to ask what God intended to say to the text's original

---

[6] For example, history, letters, apocalyptic, wisdom, poetry etc.

[7] For a thorough treatment of principles 1-3 read John R. W. Stott, *Understanding the Bible*, Anzea Books, Sydney, 1972, p 217-238.

readers. For example, determining the original meaning of 'But he was pierced for our transgressions, he was crushed for our iniquities' (Isa. 53:5a), a verse we sometimes quickly interpret as referring purely to Jesus, requires answers to the following subset of questions. Firstly, what was the historical context of Isaiah's composition? This might alert you to who the pierced and crushed one originally referred to and who they were pierced and crushed for. Secondly, what was the original meaning of the individual words (for example, what did 'iniquity' mean to an Israelite at that time?) Thirdly, what significance does the original cultural setting have for the text's meaning? This may not help in the case of Isaiah 53:5, but an understanding of the cultural customs found in some other passages might assist interpretation. For example, how should Jesus' command to wash one another's feet be interpreted in John 13:14-15? A quick glance at a commentary on John reveals that washing feet was a task normally reserved for servants and slaves in first century Palestine. An awareness of this cultural custom helps us to interpret Jesus' words about foot-washing as a command to serve each other in humility, rather than as a literal command to wash each other's feet. So these are the questions to ask, the answers to which will be found in a good Bible commentary.

3. What is the text's meaning in the context of the whole Bible?
Your interpretation of a Bible text must harmonise with all the other Bible texts because they have the same divine author. Negatively, this makes contradictory interpretations intolerable. Positively, it encourages you to use Scripture to interpret Scripture. This requires you to take the immediate literary context of your text into consideration. For example, the promises of Genesis 12:1-3 look pretty anaemic until they are interpreted within the context of what precedes (that is, the rebellion and punishment of mankind in Gen. 3–11) and what follows (that is, partial fulfillment of God's promises to Abraham in Gen. 12–50). By asking what precedes and follows this text it enables us to interpret Genesis 12:1-3 as God's promise to ultimately restore his fallen creation through Abraham's descendants.

More broadly, God's divine authorship of Scripture invites you to allow texts, from elsewhere in the Bible, to throw light on more difficult texts. For example, Jesus' requirement that you be 'born of water and Spirit', (John 3:5b), is hard to interpret without God's explanation in Ezekiel 36:25-26 that he would one day cleanse sinful hearts (through the sprinkling of water) and put a new spirit in them. So a relatively simple text from Ezekiel can help in the interpretation of a more difficult text written by John more than 600 years later. This is only possible because God authored both texts.

4. What is the relevance of the text's meaning today?

After determining your text's original meaning, you need to interpret how God expects you to respond to that meaning. What was his purpose? You write things to achieve a purpose. Even a personal diary is written for the purpose of jolting your own memory later. God intends his words to accomplish the purpose for which they were sent (Isa. 55:11). So interpretation also involves asking what the appropriate response to God's Word is. Sometimes this will be easy. John openly declares that 'these are written *that you may believe* that Jesus is the Christ' (John 20:31). But it is not always so easy to see what response God purposed his words to achieve. Begin by asking how the original readers were required to respond. For example, Ephesians 6:9 expects Christian slave masters to respond by allowing their relationship to God govern how they treat their servants. They're not to threaten their slaves, as was the norm in their society.[8] Their management practice was to reflect an awareness of their accountability to God, *the* Master of master and slave. Now ask how the modern Christian employer should respond to Ephesians 6:9. They should not manage their staff according to the *norm* of large city businesses(which may be unethical), but in a way that is acceptable to God, even when this is not the most economically efficient management practice. Fortunately, the Spirit enables the Bible to be interpreted within new contexts (John 16:13),

---

[8] See Peter T. O'Brien, *The Letter to the Ephesians*, Apollos, Leicester, 1999, p 454.

thereby encouraging you to interpret how the Bible applies to you and your listeners today.[9]

Interpreting God's Word for others 'in Christ'

Now your union with Christ has implications for how you interpret the Bible for others united with him – the church. The church is described as Christ's body on the basis of his Spirit's indwelling of believers (1 Cor. 12:12-13; Eph. 2:11-22). We don't exactly look and behave like a body of united parts now, but we will when Christ returns (1 Cor. 13:8-12; Eph. 4:13). In the meantime we must labour at conforming the church to the image of Christ, a work that requires our interpretation of the Bible for others. This will involve three things.

1. A Christ-centred approach to interpretation

Firstly, your interpretative aim must be Christ-centred. The body of Christ is to be built up (like the Christ remembered from Scripture, see Eph. 4:12-13). This is achieved by presenting the church with the image of Christ found in Scripture.

I used to research dairy cows. The aim was to 'build-up' milk production. However, we'd never tell farmers how to get more milk before we'd tested our ideas with science. We'd run all kinds of smelly experiments and present a blueprint that could be enacted with confidence – advice based on hard evidence. Scientific truth was foundational to accomplishing the aim of increasing milk production. Likewise, the aim to 'build up the body of Christ' must be based on the truth about Christ interpreted from Scripture. When interpretation fails to understand Christ from Scripture, God's aim for his church becomes displaced by your aims. At worst you might be urging others to enact the Christ of your own imagination. Don't give me another 'Home Improvement' sermon based on the latest secular self-help book. Use Christ-centred interpretation to show me how Christ would live in my home. Look at how Paul does this when writing to the Ephesians about marriage (Eph. 5:22-33). The church's submission to Christ is the model for how a wife should submit to her husband (22-24) and

---

[9] See Chapter 3 'A Method'.

Christ's love for the church is presented as the model for how a husband should love his wife (25-28).

2. Modelling interpretation for others

Secondly, you need to model interpretation for others so that they can learn to interpret for themselves. Let your interpretative method be transparent to your hearers in your preaching, group Bible studies, Scripture lessons and Sunday school talks. The current trend of sweeping across the Bible in a single sermon is unfortunate. I recently heard a sermon that used the whole Bible to explain the resurrection of believers described in 1 Corinthians 15! Surely this imposes the daunting idea upon the listener that to interpret one passage requires an understanding of the whole Bible *and* two or three commentaries. Conversely, if your talk reflects your Christ-centred interpretative aim, responsible interpretative methods and demonstrates how you have worked to crystallize the big idea of the author,[10] you will have gone a long way in modelling and encouraging people to interpret the Bible for themselves.

3. Interpreting for others who can't interpret for themselves

Thirdly, you need to interpret for those in the body of Christ who can't interpret for themselves; especially Christian children, the mentally disabled, the elderly and those from other cultures that have only recently been exposed to the Gospel. When the task of interpreting the Bible for these people is neglected, they are invited to invent how Christ might have lived in their situation.

The need to interpret all Scripture

Your union with Christ commits you to interpreting all of the Bible since it is all about him (Luke 24:15-49; John 5:39-47). Ask how each part of the Bible eventually informs and enriches your understanding of him. But how can the Old Testament be useful to my understanding of Christ? I remember Peter Adam, of Ridley College in Melbourne, explaining that the benefit of God's postponement of his Son's mission to the

---

[10] See Chapter 3 'A Method' for details on determining an author's 'big idea'.

world, after mankind's rebellion in the Garden (Gen. 3), was to build a worldview in which the full significance of Christ's person and work could be interpreted.

Think about it this way. Childbirth might be painful, but can you imagine the trauma of birthing children through the front door as adolescents? This child's grunts and groans would be met by the disappointed stares of new parents who'd have no historical background to motivate their love and acceptance of him. All this without your epidural! Alternatively, natural birth gives you a background of nappy-changing, feeding, schooling, discipline and holidays against which you can read this adolescent.

Jesus wasn't born into this world without a historical context to be received into. There was the Old Testament. Thousands of years of Israelite history follow Genesis 3. The characters of God and man come to life and God's plans for his fallen creation, which culminate in an expected Christ, are charted. But it also presents us with the God-given religion of Israel, a religion that, as it turns out, foreshadowed the person and work of Jesus Christ (Col. 2:17; Heb. 8:5; 10:1). So the resource of the Old Testament comes into your hands to ensure you receive an enriched picture of what Christ is like. Your Christ-likeness is properly understood against this background. Whatever part of the Bible you interpret, you need to ask 'How does what this author has said to those people, at that time in history, enrich my understanding of Christ and Christ-like living?'[11]

The end of interpretation
Well, those love-goggled eyes have screeched to a halt on what is the first bar of a page of scribbled musical notes! What are you to do when your beloved author writes you music? Presumably the recipient is a musician. The notes are not to be *read* for information, but *played* for transformation. He picks up his violin and plays, no, soars over them! The author has made her intended interpreter

---

[11] Space doesn't permit us to teach a method for biblical theology here. See Graeme Goldsworthy, *Preaching the Whole Bible as Christian Scripture: An Application of Biblical Theology to Expository Preaching*, Eerdmans, Cambridge, United Kingdom, 2000.

respond appropriately to what she has written. Everyone in his house has heard!

Likewise, the words of the Bible were never intended to merely convey information, but to elicit a response from their intended interpreter. God is concerned about the response you make to his words (2 Tim. 3:14-15). He is concerned that you strive to conform your life to the truth you find. That is wise interpretation: living in harmony with the text. What truth you find in interpretation should be as transformative as it is informative. And just as the violinist's performance witnessed to the content of his love letter's last page to all within hearing, so your life will witness to the texts you interpret as you are transformed by the truth about Christ – your new identity. The specific vocation of the interpreter of Scripture, the person united with Christ, is to be a true witness: 'one who not only can describe, but embody, God's communicative intent'.[12]

---

[12] Vanhoozer, *First Theology*, p 308.

5.

A METHOD OF PREPARATION

DAVID COOK

The late nineteenth century preacher Philips Brooks defined preaching as 'truth through personality'; if that is the case, then not only the talk itself but the method of preparation of the talk is as individual as one's fingerprint.

In the preparation of my Bible talks I use the enclosed pyramid method to prepare, which you might also find a helpful preparation tool. It does seem to be a method that is easily transferable.

I begin at the foot of the pyramid 'movements in the passage'. I try to isolate the main thoughts, for example in John 3:16 they would centre around the verbs – God loved – God gave – whoever believes; three movements.

The summary of the passage is really the engine room of sermon preparation. Here I summarise the passage in point form with verse references. I am careful not to add interpretive remarks in my summary; the verse reference ensures that I am saying only what is in the passage itself.

For example:

1. The Son of Man must be lifted up as the snake was in the desert (v. 14).
2. Everyone who believes in him may have eternal life (v. 15).

3. God loved the world so much that he gave his only son
   (v. 16).
4. Whoever believes in him will have life and not perish
   (v. 16).

The close parallelling of verses 15 and 16 becomes apparent, the lifting up of the snake with the lifting up of Jesus.

McNeile Dixon[1] said, 'the human mind is not as philosophers would have you think, a debating hall, but a picture gallery'. So in the dominant picture, I look for the main metaphor, or simile of the passage. It may be the tree of Psalm 1; the salt of Matthew 5; the put off/put on dynamic of Ephesians 4.

In John 3:15-16, it is the lifting up of the symbol of God's judgment on sin; the serpent at Mount Horeb; the son at the cross. The dominant picture is the elevation of the symbol of God's judgment for all to recognise.

Whatever the dominant picture is, the preacher will seek to impress this on the mind of the listener. When the listener arrives at your venue, a suitable picture may be on the overhead without explanation, its significance becoming apparent only as the talk is being given. For example, if you are preaching on Psalm 1, the picture may be of a tree. I always look for an image that gets people thinking about the text.

Haddon Robinson[2] quotes Jowett, the Pastor of Westminster Chapel, London, who was speaking at the Yale lectures on preaching, 'I have a conviction that no sermon is ready for preaching, not ready for writing out until we can express its theme in a short, pregnant sentence as clear as crystal'. Robinson calls this 'the big idea'.

To reach the big idea, first get the subject, that is, what is the writer talking about in one, two or three words.

Then the complement follows, that is, what is the writer saying about what he is talking about? Then, by putting the subject and complement together, you have the one-sentenced big idea.

---

[1] Quoted by W. W. Wiersbe *Preaching and Teaching with Imagination*, Victor Books, USA, 1994, p 24.

[2] H. W. Robinson *Biblical Preaching – the Development and Delivering of Expository Messages*, Baker Bookhouse, USA, 1980, p 35.

John 3:16

Subject (What is he talking about?): God's love.

Complement (What is he saying about what he is talking about?): God's love is seen in the gift of his son, so that the believer can have life.

Big Idea (The combination of subject and complement): God's love is seen in his gift of Jesus so that the believer can have life.

The big question which follows simply puts that statement of the big idea into the form of a question, so that every passage, and therefore every talk, is answering a question.

I like to give myself question options – Kipling said, 'six faithful men taught me everything I knew, what, when, where, why, and how and who'. [3]

The following are optional big questions for John 3:16:

What is God's love like?
Where do I see God's love?
Why did God give Jesus?
Why did Jesus die?
How can I have life?
How do I know God loves me?
Who has life?

The choosing of the big question is crucial, for if I choose a good big question which is not the question being answered by the text, then the result will be confusion in the listener. So I must choose the question and then test it against the text to make sure it is the big question which the text answers.

I'll choose as the big question for John 3:16, 'Why did God give Jesus?' The text answers – because God loves us so that we might have life through faith in Jesus.

The next question is crucial and concerns the context. I want to place my text in the context of the Bible, that is, where does its book (John's Gospel) fit into the canon of Scripture? What is its context in the flow of God's plan of salvation from

---

[3] R Kipling, *Just So Stories*, 'The Elephant's Child'.

Genesis to Revelation? Then I will fit it into the context of its own book, that is, John's Gospel.

The shorter the text, the greater the attention needed to be given to context. In this case, the context of verse 16 in what comes before, verse 15, and after, verse 17, is crucial.

All my work thus far has been between me and the text in dependence on the Holy Spirit who breathed the text out. In this early stage of preparation I try to be a commentary-free-zone, otherwise I will tend to let the commentator do the thinking for me.

'A truth taught is interesting
A truth caught is exciting and challenging
A truth discovered is life changing'

The truth I discover as I study and reflect, while depending on God, is a truth which I will speak about with a greater degree of enthusiasm and passion.

It would be foolish to ignore the wisdom of the commentary, but if consulted too early then the commentary can stifle thought and enlightenment between me and the text. Remember the listener has come to hear you, not you simply regurgitating the commentator.

Commentaries can give insight and correction. Try not to consult them until you have completed the pyramid. This will give you a clearer idea of the questions you need the commentator to answer.

The second most common criticism of expository Bible talks is that they are rarely earthed in real life; they are more like lectures than anything else. (We will deal with the most common criticism in the next chapter.) This is where application helps what the Puritans called the 'use' of the text, showing how the truth attaches or applies to life.

At the foot of the page I write down everything I learn about God and people from the text, these are the two 'unchangeables' from the text to the present. God is eternally consistent and people, though we change outwardly in many ways and reflect different cultures, at heart are still sinners, sinners as we have always been. Look for the human depravity factor – how does our sinful rebellion show itself in the text?

What does John 3:16 tell me about God? He loves; loves widely (the world); loves sacrificially (his son); and loves purposefully (gives life).

Martyn Lloyd-Jones said that all we need to know about people is what the Bible tells us.[4] What does John 3:16 tell me about us? We are loved dearly; God's purpose is that we have life; we are perishable. Human depravity factor – how does our rebellion show itself? We have a choice of life or perishing – though loved, we can still choose not to trust.

Then I work on the three different levels of application: the necessary, possible and impossible.

The 'necessary application' shows how the passage must apply without exception, to everyone at all times.

For example, in John 3:16, I must believe in Jesus to have life. The appropriate response to God's love is to trust in Jesus. The 'possible application' shows how this truth applies to me. While it may not apply to the listener in the same way, it may be helpful for them to know I must ensure that my trust is at rest in Jesus and not shifting on my own performance. So I will spend the first fifteen minutes of each day reminding myself of the gospel, through reading, prayer and singing; reminding myself that my relationship with God depends on Jesus' work, not mine.

I must not give this possible application the same weight as the necessary application, either unwittingly or purposefully pushing a helpful insight into a binding law, so that every believer must spend the first fifteen minutes of every day like I do.

Whenever I prepare a talk I try to assume the majority of the listeners are living consistently with the 'impossible application' of the passage.

In Matthew 6:24 Jesus said, 'You cannot serve both God and money'. The impossible understanding of that passage is that 'I am exceptional; I can have two masters, God and money'. I believe that the majority of listeners live consistently with

---

[4] D. Martyn Lloyd-Jones, *Preaching & Preachers*, Hodder & Stoughton, London, 1971.

the thinking that they are exceptional and can live with two masters.

I always work out the impossible application of a passage and point it out to the hearer because I think the majority of hearers privately affirm this impossible understanding of the text.

For example, in John 3:16 the 'impossible application' is that I can ignore Jesus and still not perish; or I can have life apart from a confident trust in the work of Jesus on my behalf, that my work is sufficient to earn and keep God's gift of life. These would be impossible understandings of the passage and may well be believed by the majority of our hearers.

As I have been working through the pyramid I have also been noting potential illustrations that have come to mind. On completion of the pyramid, I have noted questions that need answering, words that need more research, expressions that may not be clear, links which need to be understood and explained.

I am now ready to draft the talk. I will set it out like this:

Introduction:
Where I introduce the big question and show the listener why it is a relevant question for their life situation.

In the introduction I need to grip the listener's attention, I must never presume that I have it automatically. Simply announcing the text is not good enough, I need to respect the text by clearly explaining it, but I need to respect the listener by seeking to win their interest.

In John 3:16, the big question of the text is, 'Why did God give Jesus?' I might make my point of contact the giving of a gift and the various reasons we give gifts. I try not to speak in the abstract but talk about the gifts I have given or been given, and the reasons for them. Then to the reason God gave Jesus.

Body of the talk:
A structure of two, three or four points. The structure will usually follow the movements of the passage; if there are three movements then there will be a three-point structure. Structure is important as a memory tool, a talk without a structure is like a body without a skeleton; it also helps the rational flow of what you have to say.

Conclusion:
Here I seek to sharpen the application, seeking to move the will of the listener to repentance and faith.

I think of the talk like a 747 jumbo jet, it takes a lot of thrust to get it off the ground and a lot to get it back down, so I spend considerable time thinking about the introduction (take off) and the conclusion (landing).

I write out my manuscript in full, without the use of a computer, not exactly word for word, but close to it. I then try and produce a summary of the whole, where I underline, highlight and circle, before delivering the talk using only the summary notes.

On the following pages I have completed pyramids on Mark 10:35-45; Psalm 1 and Ephesians 5:15-21.

During preparation I always keep a couple of books near my desk, which I find help me immeasurably in preparation.

John Calvin was a great reformer and his *Institutes of the Christian Religion* many believe to be the greatest works of systematic theology written in the history of the church. I mention them because Calvin became a great theologian not for his own sake but in order to be a better pastor.

If I am going to be giving Bible talks I must continue to read systematic theology. I must always be aware of the theology being taught by my text. A good substantial work of systematic theology is important, make sure it has good biblical indexing and continues to drive you back to the Bible as its supreme authority.

The book I am using at the moment is Robert L. Reymond's *A New Systematic Theology of the Christian Faith*. Reymond has sixteen references in his book to John 3:15-16 and I will follow each of them up in order to be aware of the theological truths being raised by the text.

The other book which I find helpful, especially in application, is Jay E. Adam's *The Christian Counsellor's Manual*. Adams has good biblical indexing and has five references to John 3:16. Adams is helpful in that he shows the application of a text to various pastoral counselling situations.

I always check what Reymond and Adams have to say about the text I am preparing.

PREACHING PYRAMID

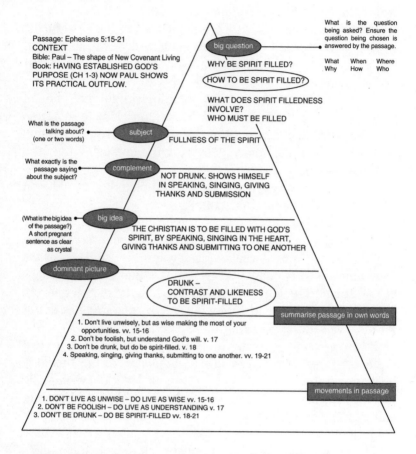

Passage: Ephesians 5:15-21
CONTEXT
Bible: Paul – The shape of New Covenant Living
Book: HAVING ESTABLISHED GOD'S PURPOSE (CH 1-3) NOW PAUL SHOWS ITS PRACTICAL OUTFLOW.

What is the question being asked? Ensure the question being chosen is answered by the passage.

What   When   Where
Why   How   Who

big question

WHY BE SPIRIT FILLED?
HOW TO BE SPIRIT FILLED?
WHAT DOES SPIRIT FILLEDNESS INVOLVE?
WHO MUST BE FILLED

What is the passage talking about? (one or two words)

subject

FULLNESS OF THE SPIRIT

What exactly is the passage saying about the subject?

complement

NOT DRUNK. SHOWS HIMSELF IN SPEAKING, SINGING, GIVING THANKS AND SUBMISSION

(What is the big idea of the passage?) A short pregnant sentence as clear as crystal

big idea

THE CHRISTIAN IS TO BE FILLED WITH GOD'S SPIRIT, BY SPEAKING, SINGING IN THE HEART, GIVING THANKS AND SUBMITTING TO ONE ANOTHER

dominant picture

DRUNK – CONTRAST AND LIKENESS TO BE SPIRIT-FILLED

summarise passage in own words

1. Don't live unwisely, but as wise making the most of your opportunities. vv. 15-16
2. Don't be foolish, but understand God's will. v. 17
3. Don't be drunk, but do be spirit-filled. v. 18
4. Speaking, singing, giving thanks, submitting to one another. vv. 19-21

movements in passage

1. DON'T LIVE AS UNWISE – DO LIVE AS WISE vv. 15-16
2. DON'T BE FOOLISH – DO LIVE AS UNDERSTANDING v. 17
3. DON'T BE DRUNK – DO BE SPIRIT-FILLED vv. 18-21

Application: (What does it tell us about)

GOD: *Will conclude the days; has a purpose; intends his people to be Spirit-filled; respects joy, thanksgiving, submission.*

US: *Make the most of opportunities, not be active without discernment; at our most godly when encouraging, giving thanks, submitting to one another.*

Necessary – (Always necessary for all people) *Be filled with the Spirit by involvement in active encouragement, expressing joy and thanksgiving and submission to one another.*

Possible – (Sometimes possible for some people) *I will seek ways of expressing encouragement, reasons for thanksgiving, and to be creative in submission within Christ's body today.*

Impossible – (How the passage cannot be applied) *To be filled with the Spirit is an experience that occurs apart from active encouragement, thankful, joyous, submissive service. The filling of the Spirit is an ethereal and abstract experience without practical implications with how I relate to others.*

PREACHING PYRAMID

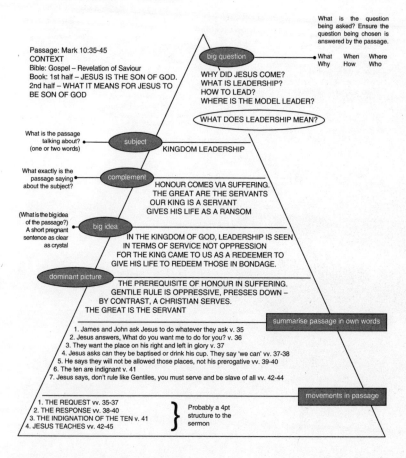

What is the question being asked? Ensure the question being chosen is answered by the passage.

What   When   Where
Why   How   Who

Passage: Mark 10:35-45
CONTEXT
Bible: Gospel – Revelation of Saviour
Book: 1st half – JESUS IS THE SON OF GOD.
2nd half – WHAT IT MEANS FOR JESUS TO
BE SON OF GOD

big question

WHY DID JESUS COME?
WHAT IS LEADERSHIP?
HOW TO LEAD?
WHERE IS THE MODEL LEADER?

WHAT DOES LEADERSHIP MEAN?

What is the passage
talking about?
(one or two words)

subject

KINGDOM LEADERSHIP

What exactly is the
passage saying
about the subject?

complement

HONOUR COMES VIA SUFFERING.
THE GREAT ARE THE SERVANTS
OUR KING IS A SERVANT
GIVES HIS LIFE AS A RANSOM

(What is the big idea
of the passage?)
A short pregnant
sentence as clear
as crystal

big idea

IN THE KINGDOM OF GOD, LEADERSHIP IS SEEN
IN TERMS OF SERVICE NOT OPPRESSION
FOR THE KING CAME TO US AS A REDEEMER TO
GIVE HIS LIFE TO REDEEM THOSE IN BONDAGE.

dominant picture

THE PREREQUISITE OF HONOUR IN SUFFERING.
GENTILE RULE IS OPPRESSIVE, PRESSES DOWN –
BY CONTRAST, A CHRISTIAN SERVES.
THE GREAT IS THE SERVANT

summarise passage in own words

1. James and John ask Jesus to do whatever they ask v. 35
2. Jesus answers, What do you want me to do for you? v. 36
3. They want the place on his right and left in glory v. 37
4. Jesus asks can they be baptised or drink his cup. They say 'we can' vv. 37-38
5. He says they will not be allowed those places, not his prerogative vv. 39-40
6. The ten are indignant v. 41
7. Jesus says, don't rule like Gentiles, you must serve and be slave of all vv. 42-44

movements in passage

1. THE REQUEST vv. 35-37
2. THE RESPONSE vv. 38-40
3. THE INDIGNATION OF THE TEN v. 41
4. JESUS TEACHES vv. 42-45

} Probably a 4pt
structure to the
sermon

Application: (What does it tell us about)

GOD: *God's King enters glory via suffering, God esteems service. God
       redeems.*

US: *We are ambitious for self and naturally oppressive.*

Necessary – (Always necessary for all people) *Resist HDF – don't be oppressive
           and self-serving. Recognise his redemption and follow the way of the
           servant King.*

Possible – (Sometimes possible for some people) *How servant leadership applies
          to us as a husband, father, employer, employee, church leader.*

Impossible – (How the passage cannot be applied) *10:36, 10:51. Instead of "What
            do you want me to do for you?" I ask "What do you want to do for me?"
            I use people in the name of Christ to serve my own ends.*

HDF = Human depravity factor

PREACHING PYRAMID

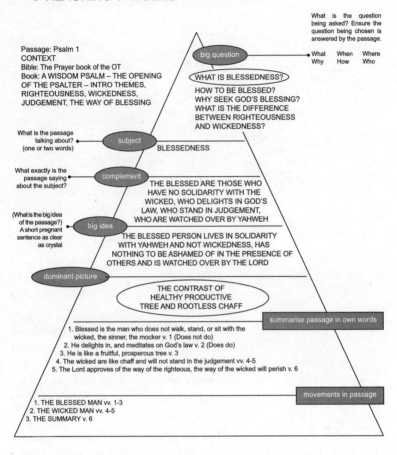

Passage: Psalm 1
CONTEXT
Bible: The Prayer book of the OT
Book: A WISDOM PSALM – THE OPENING
OF THE PSALTER – INTRO THEMES,
RIGHTEOUSNESS, WICKEDNESS,
JUDGEMENT, THE WAY OF BLESSING

What is the question being asked? Ensure the question being chosen is answered by the passage.

What   When   Where
Why   How   Who

big question

WHAT IS BLESSEDNESS?

HOW TO BE BLESSED?
WHY SEEK GOD'S BLESSING?
WHAT IS THE DIFFERENCE
BETWEEN RIGHTEOUSNESS
AND WICKEDNESS?

What is the passage talking about? (one or two words)

subject

BLESSEDNESS

What exactly is the passage saying about the subject?

complement

THE BLESSED ARE THOSE WHO
HAVE NO SOLIDARITY WITH THE
WICKED, WHO DELIGHTS IN GOD'S
LAW, WHO STAND IN JUDGEMENT,
WHO ARE WATCHED OVER BY YAHWEH

(What is the big idea of the passage?) A short pregnant sentence as clear as crystal

big idea

THE BLESSED PERSON LIVES IN SOLIDARITY
WITH YAHWEH AND NOT WICKEDNESS, HAS
NOTHING TO BE ASHAMED OF IN THE PRESENCE OF
OTHERS AND IS WATCHED OVER BY THE LORD

dominant picture

THE CONTRAST OF
HEALTHY PRODUCTIVE
TREE AND ROOTLESS CHAFF

summarise passage in own words

1. Blessed is the man who does not walk, stand, or sit with the wicked, the sinner, the mocker v. 1 (Does not do)
2. He delights in, and meditates on God's law v. 2 (Does do)
3. He is like a fruitful, prosperous tree v. 3
4. The wicked are like chaff and will not stand in the judgement vv. 4-5
5. The Lord approves of the way of the righteous, the way of the wicked will perish v. 6

movements in passage

1. THE BLESSED MAN vv. 1-3
2. THE WICKED MAN vv. 4-5
3. THE SUMMARY v. 6

Application: (What does it tell us about)

GOD: *Has a law, will judge; watches over the way of the righteous, will judge wickedness.*

US: *Be careful of what we delight in; who we show solidarity with, God has made us to be fruitful and productive, not rootless and directionless.*

Necessary – (Always necessary for all people). *Be the truly blessed person by delighting in God and showing no solidarity with the wicked.*

Possible – (Sometimes possible for some people) *Be careful of the progressive immorality of v. 1 Make sure I give time to that in which I delight.*

Impossible – (How the passage cannot be applied) *The truly blessed man is the one who does his own thing, he is a law unto himself. We are not blessed when we are in control of our own destiny. Freedom = ignoring, mocking of God and his legalistic constraints.*

6.

INTRODUCTIONS, CONCLUSIONS AND PURPOSE

JONATHAN DYKES

Composing introductions and conclusions can be the hardest part of sermon preparation. At least I think so, and I suspect many others find it the same. If you speak to someone who preaches frequently, I'm sure they'll be able to tell you about breaking out in a cold sweat the night before preaching when, try as they might, they just can't scrape a decent introduction together. They'll speak of the knuckle-gnawing desperation of rifling through their collection of newspaper and magazine clippings, old sermon notes and books, and badgering their spouse, searching for *something, anything...!*

I find it very easy when I am short on preparation time to neglect these parts of my sermon. I slip into a mindset where I think: 'they're just the window dressing anyway, they don't really matter – what counts is just the "meat" of the sermon'. When this happens I have actually begun to view the introduction and conclusion as 'add-ons' to the sermon. They are simply the parts to be stuck on the front and back of the sermon to entertain my hearers. They are the 'optional extras' – nice if you've got them, but not essential. The result is that I end up with an introduction that is superficial and has only a tenuous link to the sermon, and a conclusion that has no backbone.

As I listen to other preachers' introductions and conclusions, it strikes me that the best ones are those that are intimately connected to the purpose and the application of the sermon itself. Rather than being tenuously linked add-ons, they are integral parts of the whole. They gather up the hearer into the great theme of the sermon, they strike a nerve, they dig deep and they drive the nail home. The result is that the hearer, at the end of the introduction is not simply curious, but compelled to listen, because they know they need to hear this. At the conclusion's end, they are convicted and compelled to action and to change their lives in accordance with God's revelation.

This demonstrates that an introduction and a conclusion have a purpose. They are the means to an end, not an end in and of themselves. As this purpose is directly related to the purpose of the sermon as a whole, it is necessary to discuss this first, before we look at introductions and conclusions.

1. The importance of Purpose
General purpose

I enjoy collecting quotes about preaching. Here is one of my favourites, it is from Henry Ward Beecher:

> ...in every sermon, the preacher should propose to himself definite ends to be gained. A sermon is not like a Chinese fire-cracker, to be fired off for the noise which it makes. *It is the hunter's gun, and at every discharge he should look to see his game fall.* The power is wasted if nothing be hit.[1] [italics mine]

This captures the whole idea of preaching with purpose very succinctly. Henry Ward Beecher is talking about *taking aim.* He is talking about taking aim *at a target.* He is talking about hitting the mark *because you are aiming at an object.* He is talking about preaching with *purpose.* Understanding that each time I stand up in front of people to preach I am aiming at 'definite ends to be gained' has been a great help and encouragement to me.

---

[1] Henry Ward Beecher, *Lectures on Preaching*, T. Nelson & Sons, Paternoster Row, Edinburgh, 1872, p. 236.

If you go through the roll call of great preachers of the last 300 years and read their sermons you will realise very quickly that they all understood what it means to preach with purpose: Billy Graham, Martyn Lloyd-Jones, Charles H. Spurgeon, George Whitefield, Jonathan Edwards and John Wesley to name a few. These men knew their target, they took aim and they fired. And the Lord blessed their efforts. Listen to these words from Spurgeon:

> Your business is not merely to teach the children in your classes to read the Bible, not merely to inculcate the duties of morality, nor merely to instruct them in the mere letter of the gospel, but your high calling is to be the means, in the hands of God, of bringing life from heaven to dead souls...*Resurrection, then, is our aim! To raise the dead is our mission!*"[2]

...from Lloyd-Jones:

> What is the chief end of preaching? I like to think it is this. It is to give men and women a sense of God and His presence...I can forgive a man for a bad sermon, I can forgive the minister almost anything if he gives me a sense of God, if he gives me something for my soul, if he gives me the sense that, though he is inadequate himself, he is handling something which is very great and very glorious, if he gives me some dim glimpse of the majesty and glory of God, the love of Christ my Saviour and the magnificence of the Gospel. If he does that I am his debtor, and I am profoundly grateful to him.[3]

and from Richard Baxter:

> As one that ne'er should preach again,
> And as a dying man to dying men.[4]

---

[2] Charles H. Spurgeon, *The Soul Winner*, Christian Focus Publications, Ross-shire, 1992, p 112.

[3] D. Martyn Lloyd-Jones, *Preaching and Preachers*, Hodder & Stoughton, London, 1971, p 97.

[4] J.I. Packer, *A Quest for Godliness*, Crossway Books, Illinois, 1990, p. 288.

These men preached with urgency, with passion, with conviction and with earnestness. They were compelled, they were driven, they were absorbed, and they were 'spent' in their preaching. They all had their own 'style', but it was God's Word preached in such a way that the Holy Spirit used to convict, to urge and to compel their hearers to action, to change. They understood that preaching was *not an end in and of itself, but the means to an end* – God changing people's lives. They took their cue from the apostolic preaching, like Peter at Pentecost. It is telling that both Spurgeon and Lloyd-Jones express the purpose of preaching *in terms of the response elicited in the lives of their hearers.*

For the preacher, these are men to remember. Be like them. When you preach, preach for change: God changing people's lives.

Often the purpose of preaching is said to be 'to teach the Bible'. I believe that this is an unhelpful and inaccurate way of describing the purpose of preaching. It is unhelpful for several reasons. Firstly, if that really is the sum purpose of preaching then, technically speaking, I could stand in front of a brick wall and preach for thirty minutes and fulfil that. In other words, it is unhelpful because it is an inadequate definition. Secondly, it puts the idea into the preacher's mind that all he has to do is 'teach what the Bible says' and then sit down, his job finished. The result is that the sermon becomes a lecture. It is the contrast between what Don Carson has called preaching and 'exegetical lecturing'.[5]

Think of a lecturer in a university. Their primary purpose is to send their students out of the lecture theatre with a clear understanding of the subject at hand. The students need to know about the subject and so the lecturer needs to explain it. Or take a lecturer in a Bible College. They are intent on teaching the students what the Bible says. They can stand in front of the class, exegete the text, explain to the class what it meant to the original hearers, how it applies to life now and even illustrate all of this along the way. But are they preaching?

---

[5] Don Carson, *Katoomba Christian Convention 2003 Centenary Preaching Conference*, 'The What and Why of Expository Preaching'. This address is a very helpful discussion of what preaching really is and is well worth listening to.

Preaching is not lecturing. I believe the chief difference lies in the purpose. It is this purpose or 'element of attack' that Martyn Lloyd-Jones viewed as what marks the sermon off from the lecture:

Its appeal [a lecture] is almost exclusively to the mind; its object is to give instruction and state facts. That is its primary purpose and function. So a lecture, again, lacks, and should lack, the element of attack, *the concern to do something to the listener, which is a vital element in preaching.*[6] [italics mine]

The description of the purpose of preaching – to teach the Bible – is also inaccurate. This is because God does not describe the purpose of preaching in these terms in His Word. Once again, it is a question of distinguishing the means from the end. We should preach with the purpose of seeing God changing people's lives. That is the 'end'. The way we do that is by 'teaching the Bible'. That is the 'means' to the 'end'[7]. It may sound like a small difference in words, but it has a major impact in practice.

So the general statement of the purpose of preaching that I use is:

'To so teach the Bible, that my hearers are compelled to change in response to the demands of God's revelation."[8]

I find this helpful in my preparation in several ways. Firstly, it focuses my thoughts on my hearers as well as the text, not just the text itself. Preaching is, amongst other things, a form of communication, so I need to be always thinking about what is the best way of saying what I need to say. Secondly, it focuses my prayers on the work of the Holy Spirit in my life and in the lives of my hearers. It leads me to constantly seek his work of

---

[6] D. Martyn Lloyd-Jones, ibid, p 71.

[7] Peter Adam, *Speaking God's Words. A Practical Theology of Preaching*, IVP, Leicester, 1996, p 89. See esp. pp 87-89 entitled 'Teach the Bible or Preach the Message?' and then pp 125f.

[8] Don Carson, ibid.

conviction in their hearts, their minds and their wills. I won't only be focused on myself and how well I'm doing the job. Thirdly, it reminds me that I am completely inadequate for the task. Unless the Holy Spirit works in people's lives, no real, lasting change will take place.

The specific nature of the change you are seeking

In terms of the specific nature of the change you are seeking in people's lives, that will depend upon a combination of factors such as the specific situation or 'context' you are preaching in, your text and your hearers.

For example, if I am preaching to a Christian congregation – people who have been born again, regenerated – then I will be mindful that the purpose of the meeting is to gather together as brothers and sisters in the Lord Jesus Christ and hear what God has to say. So, mindful of this and my general purpose in preaching, I will choose a text (or perhaps have been given a text), seeking to edify, build, feed and grow my hearers as God's people. Then in my preparation, I will ask myself questions such as, 'Why did God include this in his Word?', 'What was the purpose of the author in writing this?'; 'What did he expect or want his readers/hearers to do as a result of this revelation?' This helps me to determine the purpose of the text. When I have figured this out I think about my hearers and connect the two. I ask myself, 'What change in my life and my hearer's life does this demand?' The answer to that question identifies the specific nature of the change required. That response in my hearers is then what I preach for.[9]

Alternatively, I may be preaching to people who are not Christians. If I am speaking at venues like a restaurant, a pub or a barbeque in someone's backyard, I will be mindful that the intent of the meeting is to preach the gospel to non-Christians. I will put my general statement of purpose together with the specific purpose of the meeting. I'm preaching for God's change in their lives and the specific nature of the change to be sought in the lives of non-Christians is that they be born

---

[9] Haddon Robinson has a very useful chapter on this in *Biblical Preaching*, Baker, Grand Rapids, Michigan, 1980, p 107.

again. Jesus Christ came to seek and save the lost (Luke 19:10 – a very clear statement of purpose!) and that should be my priority as well. Therefore, my specific aim is to preach for their conversion. Conversion is the work of the Holy Spirit, he brings it about, and for my part I must preach for it. That's the target, so that's what I'll aim for. In these instances, I will choose a text (it's unlikely I will have been given one) that takes me directly to the gospel.

Of course, in most settings there will be a mix of people – Christians and non- Christians. What you need to do is decide who you are primarily speaking to. For example, in a Christian congregation you should determine to speak primarily to the Christians (unless it is a guest service) but to do so in a way that is open, simple, accessible and clear to the people who are not Christians. If you are preaching to a gathering where the Christians have bought their non-Christian friends along to hear the gospel, then speak to the people who aren't Christians! Aim the sermon at them! Don't end up speaking primarily to the Christians! The reason they are there is for the sake of their lost friends and they want YOU to preach to those friends. They will 'listen in' while you do it, being reminded of the great truths of the gospel, being shown how to make the gospel plain to people, being shown how to demonstrate to people that they need the gospel, rejoicing that their friend is hearing it and, hopefully, praying all the time you are preaching that God will have mercy on their friend. In this situation, you are *in partnership* with your brothers and sisters, working to save the lost. Either way, you need to determine very clearly who you are speaking to. It is very difficult to do both to the best of your ability at the same time. The result may be what has been likened to dropping lemon meringue pie – it 'will splatter over everything, but hit nothing very hard'.[10]

In summary, then, a helpful way of describing your purpose as a preacher is 'to so teach the Bible that my hearers are compelled to change in response to the demands of God's revelation'. I think once a preacher realises that he is there, before God and people to 'be the means in the hands of God,

---

[10] ibid, p 107

of bringing life to dead souls' it transforms the shape and cast of the sermon as a whole and transforms the act of preaching itself. It kills our apathy and complacency in preparation, it drives us to our knees in humility and prayer; it gives us an intensity, a seriousness, and an earnestness when we preach. It gives us cause to look for and long for and grow desperate for the work of the Holy Spirit. It makes us despair of ever really being able to truly preach like we should. It enables us to ascribe all honour and glory to God himself, and him alone, for what happens.

2. Introductions
Surfacing a need

So where does that get us in terms of introductions and conclusions?

Once I have determined the purpose of the sermon, then I am in a position to consider what kind of introduction and conclusion I need. That is, the introduction and conclusion should be related to the *sermon's purpose*, not just to its *subject matter*.

For example, I might be preaching Luke 12:13-21 (the Rich Fool) to non-Christians. I could give an introduction about being rich, about what it may be like to be extremely wealthy, to want for nothing; perhaps include some stories about people who are very wealthy and the things they say and do; perhaps comment upon how we use wealth as security. Some of these things could be very attention grabbing and that is helpful. But if that is *all* my introduction does, then it is only related to my *subject matter*.

I could improve my introduction substantially by developing it to relate to my *sermon's purpose*; that is, to see my listeners converted. So I could *add* some observations about the way we define success, and ask: 'Are those definitions right in the end? Are we playing by the right rules? What if what we think is success actually isn't success? What then? What if you could look into the future and see that what you are living for now is worthless? What would you do? You'd change course, wouldn't you...?'

At that point I have touched upon my purpose (as well as my subject matter). That is useful, because then I can carry the 'tenor' of the introduction all the way through the sermon to the conclusion. Once I've got people, I don't want to let them go. It also means I've got my hearers to a point where they are more than simply curious about what I am going to say. They will hopefully be asking themselves questions like 'What if I am on the wrong track? What if I've missed what true success is? What will happen to me?' And at that point I have touched upon a need.

I remember hearing Haddon Robinson speak at a preaching conference, and he said this: 'In an introduction you have to get people's attention; to get their attention you have to get their interest; to get their interest you have to surface a need'.

That is exactly what the best sermon introductions do. They surface a need. When that happens, the hearer is compelled to listen, *because they know they need the answer.* So, in my preparation I ask myself questions such as 'Why should my hearers listen to this? Why is this important to them? What difference does it make to life – mine, theirs? How does it impact the way I think, act, feel? What great issues, joys and dilemmas of life does it touch upon?' These questions get my thoughts turning over, and they are closely linked to the application of the sermon as well. If I've worked out the nature of the change I am seeking in people's lives and my application too, then I have more food for thought for my introduction.

Sometimes we are wary of talking about 'needs'. Expressions like 'felt needs' or 'perceived needs' spring to mind. Or we say that this sort of thing is about *'making* the Bible relevant' with the implication being that we are twisting Scripture to say something it doesn't. The net result is that we shy away from surfacing 'need' in our sermons. This is an unhelpful development. The preacher's job is not to 'make the Bible relevant'; it is to work very hard at demonstrating to the hearer that it *IS relevant.* Far too often we hide behind the 'make the Bible relevant' tag and use it as an excuse for not doing the job we are meant to be doing. It is a question of knowing *what* we have to say, and then working out *how* to say it. Jesus said, 'For I did not speak of my own accord, but the Father who sent me commanded me *what* to say and *how* to say it' (John 12:49) [italics mine].

71

Exegete the text, exegete the world

The need to demonstrate the relevance of the text highlights the importance of the preacher being able to bridge the gap between 'the Bible's world' and the world of their hearer. They must not only be able to exegete the text, but be able to exegete the world around them. They must study the Scriptures and study the world. The preacher needs to be able to discern the hearer's 'worldview' – beliefs about life, the universe and everything; to really listen to the opinions being stated and questions being asked. He/she needs to pay attention to the worldviews being expressed in modern culture, in the news media, cinema, literature and music. It is this kind of knowledge and awareness that enables the preacher to effectively demonstrate very clearly and obviously the Bible's relevance to the hearer.

I have heard the analogy used of two islands and a bridge to illustrate this idea. The preacher is on his island with the 'treasure' (the Word of God), but the people he is trying to communicate with, his hearers, live on a separate island. Therefore, he must build a bridge to the other island, cross it, and persuade them to come back across to his island to look at the treasure.

It illustrates the importance of bridge building. If you don't do it, the only people you will reach are those already on your own island. If you do it, do it well. There's no point building a bridge that only reaches half-way. It might get you closer, but it still doesn't connect. In Australia today, people are moving further and further away from the truth of God's Word, even in our Sunday congregations. Therefore, we need to be putting the hard yards in to building bridges that connect.

The best place to do this is in your introduction.

A conversation?

Another way I sometimes think about my introduction is as the beginning of a conversation. I ask myself 'If this sermon was a conversation with someone, where would I begin it?' 'How would I engage someone in conversation about this, with this (my) purpose in mind?' As with all conversations in which you are seeking to share God's Word, the starting point is important, *but what is really crucial is where you take the conversation.*

That is why some people are very good at personal evangelism. They can take any topic of conversation and use it as an entry point to the gospel.

This can be a helpful tip when you are trying to put an introduction together. How can you begin this 'conversation' with your hearers in a way that will enable you to drive toward the truth you need to tell them? How can you take the things of their world, which they know and are familiar with, and move them from the 'known' to the 'unknown'? News items, personal conversations, statistics, quotes from books you have read, biographical accounts, personal observations and so on, are all useful tools.

In summary, the onus is firmly on the preacher in a sermon to demonstrate to the hearers that the Bible does have something crucial to say; in this the introduction is a key element.

3. Conclusions

No one likes a long conclusion. In high school I had an English teacher who, when asked how long our essays had to be, would reply 'As long as they need to be to answer the question'. That was good advice. Your sermon as a whole, and your conclusion, should only be as long as you need them to be to do the job.

The conclusion gathers up the main thrust of the sermon and drives it home. It brings the purpose of the sermon to a head, in all its fullness and clarity; in all its intensity and urgency. It should not be the only place in the sermon where the purpose is seen, because your application along the way should have demonstrated that as well. It is, however, the place where you focus all that you have said into a simple compelling point, and call upon and urge your hearers to respond to it.

This can be done in many ways. You may come back to a question you raised in your introduction and state clearly and explicitly how the text answers it. It is where you state, in no uncertain terms, the 'answer' to the 'problem' or 'issue' you have raised in the introduction. Hopefully your application has dealt with the issue along the way, piece by piece, but in the conclusion you put all those pieces together and gather up all the threads.

You may have found part of a hymn, some poetry, a quotation from a sermon of a great preacher, a quotation from another Christian, an extract from a famous speech, even an epitaph from someone's tombstone that captures the very essence of what you have been saying and encapsulates the desired response. If it's a hymn, have the congregation sing it to conclude the meeting. If it moves the hearer to action, use these things well.

You may know a story that will have a similar effect. An episode from the biography of a Christian missionary for example, can often be a very powerful illustration of the cost of discipleship and commitment to serving Jesus Christ with all we have. You may know a fictional story that can be used to focus people's hearts and minds on eternity, and the importance of living for his 'well done'. Tell the story well, and then wrap it up with a short punchy sentence that makes its meaning obvious to all. Some stories may not even need this.

You may finish the sermon with a stream of interrogative questions, rhetorical questions, searching questions, such as: 'Are you...?', 'Do you....?', 'Have you...?', 'Will you...?', 'Would you...?' These questions can be quite forceful (so use them carefully and well) and they are intrinsically persuasive. There is something 'uncomfortable' for the hearer about searching questions. They should be carefully weighted in a way that demands a particular self-evident answer. Don't let them be ambiguous![11] Of course, such questions can be used elsewhere in your sermon, not only in a conclusion.

You might finish with a list of action points, some necessary for everyone; others possible for people depending upon their circumstances. If you are preaching to non-Christians, then you will want to be sure to issue the challenge of the gospel to them and call them to respond then and there. It may be they have questions to ask – tell them to ask them now. They may want a Bible to read – tell them to take one now. They may

---

[11] John Carrick, *The Imperative of Preaching*. A Theology of Sacred Rhetoric, Banner of Truth, Edinburgh, 2002, p 79. This book compares the preaching devices of Jonathan Edwards, George Whitefield, Samuel Davies, Asahel Nettleton and Martyn Lloyd-Jones, giving examples from their preaching.

want to talk to someone about their problems – tell them to come and talk to someone now. They may be ready to repent and believe and need to pray with someone – tell them to do it now. Don't get them to tick a box and then send them home! Give them the opportunities they need.

The real focus of the conclusion then is to drive home the truth to the hearer so that it convinces the mind, moves the heart and quickens the will. Don't go on and on, and don't add any new ideas.

To conclude!

Method in preaching is a helpful thing, but it isn't everything. Preaching isn't simply a matter of getting the formula right, or joining the dots. It is nothing if the Holy Spirit is not involved. Just because you've prepared a great sermon doesn't necessarily mean anyone is going to understand it or be changed by it. That is the work of the Holy Spirit. I find the constant temptation in preaching is to rest and depend upon my method. If I get the right 'angle' and use the latest communication techniques and aides it will be a sure fire hit. I'm dreaming. Real change, real fruit comes from the power and work of the Holy Spirit.

Frank Retief's recent address 'Clarity in Preaching' at the *Katoomba Christian Convention Centenary Preaching Conference* addresses this issue head on.[12] It is a word in season for preachers in these days of 'talks', 'presentations' and Power-Point. You need to listen to it.

I'll leave you with one more of my favourite quotes:

> The great want of today is a holier ministry. We do not need more stalwart polemics, more mighty apologists, or preachers who encompass a wide range of natural knowledge, important though these be. But we need men of God who bring the atmosphere of heaven with them to the pulpit and speak from the borders of another world.[13]

---

[12] Frank Retief, *Katoomba Christian Convention 2003 Centenary Preaching Conference*, 'Clarity in Preaching'.

[13] Anonymous quote cited in Arturo G. Azurda III, *Spirit Empowered Preaching*, Mentor, Great Britain, 2003, p 16.

7.

APPLYING THE TEXT TO THE LISTENERS

JOHN C. CHAPMAN

Preaching is an exacting craft. When it is done well it belies the effort required to get it to a high standard. It appears to be so effortless. The preacher is in complete command of the material. It is so ordered that listening is a pleasure. The hearers are left in no doubt as to the action that they should take. Some people may even say 'He's a born preacher. It just simply pours out of him'. He, on the other hand, knows that it is nothing of the sort. It is achieved through hard work.

There are three areas that need attention if the sermon is to have its maximum impact on the listeners. They are the text of Scripture, the way the sermon is packaged, and the application.

1. The text of Scripture
Because preachers are convinced that the Scriptures are the Word of God, then much of the preparation time is used in studying the text. Preachers want to be sure that they have properly understood its meaning. It is not possible to explain something clearly unless the person explaining it understands it with clarity. The first rule of teaching is that 'the teacher must understand that which is being taught'. Confusion in the pulpit will result in thick fog in the pews.

2. The packaging
Having worked at the text of Scripture until its meaning is clear the next step is to present the material for preaching, and in such a way that it will have maximum impact on the hearer.

3. The application
The preacher is mindful of the Scripture that says that 'man does not live on bread alone but on every word that comes from the mouth of God' (Deut. 8:3; Matt. 4:4). He is to present the material so that the hearers know what action they should take or at least how to determine what action to take as a result of hearing this Scripture expounded.

When all these areas function well it will look like this:

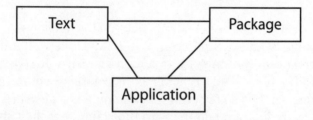

All three areas are functioning harmoniously.

However, sometimes all the effort and energy goes into the text of Scripture and, because of time constraints, the other two areas are neglected.

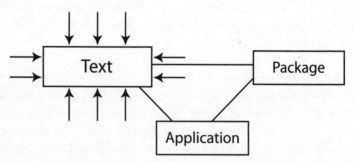

When this happens, the sermon will be harder to listen to, because little time has been spent in the packaging. The application will be reduced to something like 'Let us pray that God will do this for us'.

78

When all the effort and energy is put into the packaging

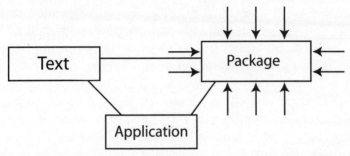

then the text gets scant attention and the application is neglected. Such a sermon might be highly entertaining, very enjoyable, and easy to listen to – but will not be life changing.

When all the effort and energy is put into the application

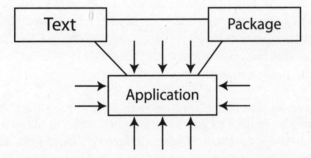

then the text and the packaging are neglected. There will be much exhortation to action but the hearer will not be able to understand why this action is called for.

What is application?
After the sermon that Peter preaches on the day of Pentecost we are told of the reaction by the people who heard it:

> ...they were cut to the heart and said to Peter and the other apostles, 'Brothers what shall we do?'
> Peter replied 'Repent and be baptized...'
> With many other words he warned them; and he pleaded with them, 'Save yourselves from this corrupt generation' (Acts 2:37-38; 40).

Application is answering the question, 'What must I do?' Because of the nature of the Word of God, action will always be required. We never come to the Bible simply to gain information as an end in itself. It is always with a view to getting to know God better and knowing how to react to him in obedience. This is well summed up in the phrase, 'Today, if you hear his voice, do not harden your hearts...' (Ps. 95:7-8).

The writer of Hebrews uses this very passage to exhort his hearers not to disregard what he has been teaching them. They are to take action and he describes it like this, 'See to it, brothers, that none of you has a sinful, unbelieving heart that turns away from the living God' (Heb. 3:12).

Repentance and faith

As Paul is travelling back to Jerusalem, at the end of his last missionary journey, he arrives at Miletus. From there he sends for the elders of the church in Ephesus to meet with him. They are to carry on the work, which he has started. He has set them an example, so he reminds them of this. Among other things Paul tells them of the response he was looking for when he preached to them.

> You know that I have not hesitated to preach anything that would be helpful to you but have taught you publicly and from house to house. I have declared to both Jews and Greeks that they must turn to God in repentance and have faith in our Lord Jesus' (Acts 20:20-21).

It might be worth noting that the response he looked for in the Jews was exactly the same response from the Gentiles although his initial approach seems to be different.[1] Also what he did privately was the same as when he did it publicly. His pastoring was the same as his preaching. There was not tension at this point.

When he writes to the church at Thessalonica, Paul reminds them of their reaction to the gospel he preached to them. Since he describes it as a model response we can take it to be

---

[1] Contrast Acts 13 and 17.

a good definition of repentance and faith. They 'turned to God from idols to serve the living and true God, and to wait for his Son from heaven, whom he raised from the dead – Jesus, who rescues us from the coming wrath' (1 Thess. 1:9-10).

The way we begin in the Christian life, is the way we proceed. This has made me wonder if there should always be a 'repentance and faith component' in every sermon as part of the application. Let me try and illustrate this:

Suppose you were preaching on the parable in Luke 18:1-8 of the persistent widow. The application is fairly clear since we are told why Jesus told the parable in the first place. It is stated in verse 1 that it was to 'show them that they should always pray and not give up'. If I apply the 'repentance and faith' principle, I will call on the hearer to repent of prayerlessness and to trust that God will hear and answer their prayers (that is, to bring justice to his chosen ones, v. 7).

Often the application is written into the text of Scripture for us. Chapters 1 and 2 of Colossians give the theological under-girding for the behaviour described in Chapters 3 and 4. The big challenge is to know how to preach it. If we are working our way systematically through the epistle, the time spent on Chapters 1 and 2 may sound like unattached doctrine. When we finally get to Chapters 3 and 4 we may be asking a lot of the congregation to remember the arguments of three weeks ago before we reach the application. Should we do both at once? That would be a great challenge.

Hebrews reads like a series of sermons linked together. The writer regularly presses his readers to take appropriate action concerning the truths of which he has just reminded them. It is a good exercise to read it and to see how often he does this and the way he does this.

When there is no immediate application given in the text the preacher needs to fill in, to the best of his/her ability, what action they think is appropriate. This application cannot have the authority of the Bible nor should it be commanded of people as if the preacher is God. We don't know what is in the heart of each person, as God does. However, I would like the preacher to tell me what action he/she is taking in response to the text.

A final word of warning

The application is not a free-for-all for the preacher to 'let fly' with their latest or oldest 'hobbyhorse'. Whatever we do, the sermon we preach MUST convey the meaning and 'push' that the original writer intended.

If it were possible for the writer to be in the congregation listening to our sermon, we ought not to surprise him with the way we have handled his work. Nothing could be better than to hear him say 'that is exactly what I meant!'

8.

ILLUSTRATION

DAVID COOK

Two of the most common criticisms of expository Bible talks are that they are not earthed in real life, being too much like a lecture; and that they are boring, what Klaas Runia calls, 'the most crushing criticism of all'.[1] No speaker can afford to neglect illustration; many congregations have been transformed from apathy to interest, from drooping eyelids to wrapped attention, simply because the speaker began to tell a story.

Illustrations have been called 'the windows of the sermon'. Bishop J. C. Ryle said, 'If you would attain simplicity in preaching you must use plenty of anecdotes and illustrations'.[2]

Others have said assertions are like feathers, they don't stand up by themselves; illustrations provide the necessary support to our statements and explanation.

Why are illustrations so helpful?

- They add interest and give relief to both you the speaker and your listener.

---

[1] K. Runia. *The Sermon Under Attack*, Paternoster Press, United Kingdom, 1983.

[2] J.C. Ryle. Talk in *The Upper Room*, ch 3 'Simplicity in Preaching", Banner of Truth, London, 1970.

- Properly used they make the truth memorable. When the illustration has been tied closely to its truth then the illustration brings the truth to mind.
- They reduce fuzziness in you the speaker. In order to use an illustration effectively you must have a clear understanding of the truth you want illustrated. The late Principal of Sydney's Moore College, Dr D. B. Knox, used to say that one doesn't understand a truth until one can put it another way. An illustration is really another way of putting a truth.
- Illustrations reveal the human side of you. You are not the neuter person, people haven't come to listen to a talking head but to a real person with hopes, fears, interests, and loves and they want to know how the truth works out in your life.

Can illustrations be dangerous?

Some speakers are so sensitive to the dangers of illustration that they don't illustrate at all. Some of the dangers include:

- The illustration is so good that it dominates. I heard a speaker once begin a talk – 'I'm about to show you something you've never seen before and will never see again'. He then peeled a banana and ate it. That was over thirty years ago, I still remember it but haven't any idea what he was illustrating.

  Illustrations must be self-effacing, like John the Baptist, pointing away from themself to the truth. It is the truth which must be prominent not the illustration.
- There are too many illustrations, so that the talk is a long string of stories one after another. Such talks will have no substance and will lack any value.
- An illustration can be inappropriate; the speaker inserts it just to keep people awake or entertained. Jokes are like this as they tend to be manipulative and are rarely appropriate. I am not against humour but a joke can detract from your overall message.
- Illustrations that are irrelevant or insensitive to your audience. When preparing your talk, take note of who

you will be speaking too – males and/or females, young people, older people or a mix.

- Illustrations taken from popular culture, such as a movie or book, and used without careful clarification, can be seen as an endorsement of the product. Don't be tempted to use a 'good bit' from an otherwise unsavoury movie or book. If the mention of a movie is going to cause your audience to fixate on it rather than your talk, don't use it.

  By getting the facts in a story wrong, your integrity and trustworthiness can be affected. If you can't get the known facts right, how can you be trusted in areas where your facts can't be checked? This is particularly the case with scientific or medical stories.

- On one occasion I began a talk by mentioning the Amalgamated Metal Workers' Union (AMWU). Afterwards, a man came up and corrected me – it was the Amalgamated Metal Workers' and Shipwrights' Union (AMWSU); he had heard nothing of my talk after that initial error.

- Illustrations can have a tendency to displace explanation of the text. In your talk the text and clear explanation must be the priority, never illustrate before you have thoroughly explained. Your illustrations should support your explanation, not take its place.

When to use illustration?

From the opening words, your talk must be designed to grip the attention of your audience. Never assume interest. Give time therefore to preparing an introduction that people will find interesting and compelling.

What types of illustrations are there?

1. Your experiences

The late Jungle Doctor, Paul White, said that to truly describe a scene you must tell me what you see, hear, feel and smell; that is what brings an illustration to life. Your ability to paint a picture your audience can not only see but imagine themself a part of, is greatly enhanced if you are describing something you have personally experienced.

Illustrations using personal encounters can be the most memorable. You may respond that nothing interesting ever happens to you, but this is not true, you just need to stop and take notice!

Tony Morphett, a scriptwriter, once came to my church in the country to speak at a dinner. That morning I picked him up from the airport and asked what he wanted to do for the day. 'My interests', he said 'are omnivorous!' We went to the Narrabri cattle sale yards, to a cotton gin and to a cotton property. All the way Tony had his notebook out taking notes.

As a communicator your interests are omnivorous; get interested even in things that don't naturally interest you.

Sometimes, if nothing seems to have happened in your experience, you'll need to make something happen. For example, I was giving a talk on Psalm 119:96, 'To all perfection I see a limit, but your commands are boundless'. I was trying to illustrate that God's Word is exceptional, because in life the older something gets, the more it depreciates. The only exceptions being God's Word and, I thought, wine.

Knowing nothing about wine I rang the Wine Society and was put through to an expert. I noted his name, always important when you don't know what you are talking about, and was told that wine also depreciates with time, the problem being corkage. Therefore God's Word is the only exception to the rule that everything depreciates with time.

There was no need to invent a story. By getting on the phone and talking to an expert, I made a story happen. You can do the same.

2. The experiences of others

A popular and effective form of illustrating is to use stories that are the experience of others; that is why biographies should always be on the reading list of the speaker. Listen and read about the experiences of others, and retell it, not as your own experience but as theirs.

A friend of mine was at a private dinner in the United States where Dr Billy Graham was present. Dr Graham was at the far end of the table and my friend could not get to speak to him. When Dr Graham left the room my friend followed him and asked if there were particular lessons the great evangelist had learnt that my friend could pass on to others in Australia.

'Yes', said Dr Graham. (Note: I am now relaying someone else's experience to you – and you can now relay it to others.) 'I should have spent more time in the Bible, more time in prayer and more time with my family'.

Such an incident has strong illustrative value.

Dr James Stewart, the late Professor of New Testament at New College in Edinburgh, called volumes of sermon illustrations the last refuge of a bankrupt intelligence. I agree with that assessment; personal discovery through your own reading, talking to people, making the links for yourself between experience and the truth is a much better way of trawling for illustrations than by using any internet-copied or printed list.

Quotes can detract from the authority of your own proclamation if you are, like the rabbis of Jesus' day, always quoting someone else. If someone has said something that has been published, then in your talk you can repeat it without having to attribute it; it's a talk you're giving, not a footnoted essay. However, if the source is significant, then attribute your quote.

Only using quotes that you can memorise ensures they are not too long and might stay in the mind of the hearers.

The founder of the WEC mission, C. T. Studd, who gave up a huge inheritance in the UK to be a missionary in India, China and Africa, when asked why, said, 'If Jesus Christ be God and died for me then no sacrifice can be too great for me to make for him'. That quote ought to be memorised and attributed because of the significance of the one who said it and of the question he was answering.

3. Observations from life

Look around at the created order, observe salt losing its saltiness, how long it takes, how it happens; look at the bee without its sting; look at how a seed quickly germinates in the soil then shrivels in the heat.

Note things that annoy you like sticky tags on fruit; people who don't have their fare ready when getting on the bus; being in the slow queue at a tollway; or garbage trucks early in the morning.

Observe life, watch people, listen to them on the train, take notes, and get them talking about their interests.

Recently I talked to a retired detective who told me that the three major causes of murder are lust, greed and revenge. He said that 98% of murders take place within five kilometres of the victim's home – miscellaneous facts but who knows when they will be useful in some Bible talk?

Some hints about gathering and harvesting stories

Get yourself a good notebook – I prefer one with an alphabetical division. Then determine your filing categories – this is an important step because you need to accurately file your stories so that you can readily harvest them when needed.

So I have a notebook for keeping stories and for each category in the notebook, I also have a separate file in the filing cabinet, for larger articles. In the notebook and file I have a category for every book of the Bible and each of the major doctrines of the faith such as God; Bible; Jesus Christ – his person and work; the Holy Spirit – his person and work; Humanity; Church; Eschatology and so on.

I'll have categories for Easter; Christmas; Cults; Counselling issues – e.g. fear, jealousy, worry; Discipleship – e.g. growth, obedience, assurance; Family issues – e.g. marriage, divorce, sex; Isms – e.g. materialism, atheism, pacifism.

I have about one hundred major categories and another two hundred sub categories within these. And I'll have a large 'miscellaneous' category for stories and clippings that just don't fit anywhere else. For example, I was speaking at a dinner in Canberra and talking about growing up in Australia in the 1950's and how my parents loved the Liberal Prime Minister, Robert Gordon Menzies.

After the dinner a man came up to me to agree that many people loved Menzies including his parents who named him Robert Gordon after Menzies. But they couldn't control his surname; it was Robert Gordon Keating[3]! While the use of that story is not immediately apparent, I have noted it and filed it under category 'God' – sub category 'Name'. Or I could just leave it in 'miscellaneous'.

---

[3] Robert Gordon Menzies and Paul Keating were Australian Prime Ministers from opposite sides of the Political Spectrum

I was interviewing an applicant for Bible College; he flipped open his diary and a purple show sash fell out. I asked him what it was for and he unfurled the Sydney Royal Easter Show sash for the Champion Duck. I asked what made a champion duck and he was full of descriptions, here was a man who knew his subject. This story stayed under 'miscellaneous' but was used at a wedding talk – What makes a champion duck? What makes a champion marriage? Let's see what God says in Genesis 2:24. Category 'Family' sub category 'Marriage', therefore becomes its permanent home.

Don't neglect the Bible as a wonderful source of illustrative material.

- The Lord as rock and refuge
- Jesus the Lamb of God; Servant King, the Good Shepherd, the True Vine, the Light of the World
- The Bible as strong meat, milk, sweeter than honey
- Death as a beaten enemy. The church as a building, branch, bride
- The Holy Spirit as a parallel helper and co-witness
- The preacher as ambassador, watchman, herald, steward
- The gospel as a momentous announcement
- The death of Jesus as redemptive and propitiatory
- The put off/put on dynamic of godliness in Ephesians 4
- The armour of God in Ephesians 6
- Prayer as a bold waking of the sleeping neighbour in Luke 11
- The shrewd stewardship of the crooked manager in Luke 16
- The huge demand of law confronting the scribe in the story of the Good Samaritan, Luke 10 – the identity of the neighbour to be loved cannot be limited

No wonder C. S. Lewis said, 'All our truth or all but a few fragments, is won by metaphor'.[4]

When you find a good story, use it well by including it in your introduction, reminding the audience of it in the body of your talk, and then concluding with it. Of course, if you

---

[4] Cited in W.W. Wiersbe, *Preaching and Teaching with Imagination*, Victor Books, 1994, p 45.

speak regularly to the same audience, you can only use the illustration once, or at least only rarely, with a big break in between.

I recently heard a sermon on 2 Corinthians 6 in which Paul's commitment to the gospel ministry was likened to the commitment of the late Laurie Nichols to the Balmain Tigers football team. The speaker mentioned his own love for the Balmain team and opened the talk with reference to Laurie, and he referred back to Laurie in the middle and at the conclusion. He could only use that illustration once with our audience and he used it most effectively.

Major newspapers, such as *The Sydney Morning Herald* and *The Age* have invaluable sections on contemporary thought and philosophy, literature reviews and cartoons.

I know a preacher who searches for old copies of the *Reader's Digest* from second-hand book shops. In well out-of-date Digests he finds a great source of material.

Time and the Australian *Bulletin* magazines can provide good material, but for contemporary comment I have found none better than a magazine entitled *World* (www.worldmag.com)

I find the *Banner of Truth* magazine (www.banneroftruth.org) thought provoking and edifying, and the monthly editorials very helpful.

There is an interesting adventist Ministerial Association, which I have used in several talks (PO Box 201 Warburton VIC 3799). The *Books and Culture Review* is well worth the subscription (www.booksandculture.com).

This week I visited my dentist and doctor. My dentist told me I needed root canal therapy and gave me pamphlets to explain the procedure. I put them aside saying I would prefer to have the experience first and then the knowledge of it later – I am a coward.

That's the way it is in the Christian life – we experience regeneration before we know what has happened to us. Our response comes after God's work; our reception and belief in his name is preceded by the 'birth from above'. John 1:12-13. File under 'Holy Spirit' sub category, 'regeneration'.

Then I visited my doctor who had a bottle of diet cola on his desk. 'I thought that was carcinogenic?' I said.

'Only if you're a rat', he replied.

File under 'miscellaneous'!!

9.

PREACHING TO THE HEART

GRANT THORP

The need for passion
The premise of this chapter is that good preaching requires passion, meaning that it will involve more than an appeal to the mind; it will also appeal to the heart and emotion. The justification of that premise is the fact that in the Bible, truth, personality and relationship are not divorced. Truth is always contextualized in a relationship and therefore is fundamentally emotional. In fact, if truth is not understood emotionally, it is not understood!

There is a deep suspicion of emotional preaching within the evangelical world. The reasons for this are varied. Some share the concern of Jonathan Edwards, whose critique of the emotionalism which broke out during the Great Awakening is still influential.[1] Others of us can perhaps remember the simple diagram we grew up with, of the train of faith pulling along the carriages of facts and feelings in that order. Still others

---

[1] Edwards in his work *On Religious Affections* sought to stress that signs of emotionalism, in and of themselves were not signs of God's work in a person's life. He stressed that, 'The ways are many whereby person's affections may be moved without any supernatural influence; the natural springs of the affections are various and secret.' The true sign of God's work in a person's life was godliness of character.
The Works of Jonathan Edwards. Banner of Truth Trust, Edinburgh, 1990, p 336.

are suspicious of emotion because of what they see happening within Pentecostal and Charismatic circles. Whatever the reason for our concern, the concern itself is that emotions can catch us up and carry us on in ways that are unhelpful, and will not last. It needs to be acknowledged that such a concern is valid. But if in reaction to that concern we neglect emotions altogether, we will fall into a cold sterile orthodoxy and our communication will lack passion and conviction.

Kierkegaard, the philosopher, said, 'My complaint is not that the age is wicked. Rather it is that it is paltry. It lacks passion'. We need to ensure that a complaint like that can't be levelled at our preaching of the gospel! Many of the great preachers of the past have commented on the need for passion in preaching. Charles Spurgeon in his *Lectures to My Students* said, 'We must not talk to our congregations as if we were half asleep. Our preaching must not be articulate snoring'.[2] Campbell Morgan, the great English congregational preacher said that the three essentials of a sermon are 'truth, clarity and passion'.[3] And in his book on preaching, the great Welsh preacher Martyn Lloyd-Jones asks, 'What is preaching?' His answer is:

Logic on fire! Eloquent reason! Are these contradictions? Of course they are not. Reason concerning the truth ought to be mightily eloquent, as you see in the case of the Apostle Paul and others. It is theology on fire. And a theology which does not take fire, I maintain, is a defective theology, or at least the man's understanding of it is defective. Preaching is theology coming through a man who is on fire.[4]

If you want to effectively communicate the gospel, then passion is not optional. It is essential. It is essential because emotion is an inherent part of the world, its inhabitants and its Creator.

---

[2] (*Cited*) J. R. W. Stott, *I Believe in Preaching*. Hodder and Stoughton, London, 1982, p 275.

[3] (*Cited*) ibid, p 284.

[4] M. Lloyd-Jones, *Preaching and Preachers*, Hodder & Stoughton, London, 1981, p 97.

Emotion everywhere

People experience the world emotionally. If you pick up any newspaper, or watch the news on television, they are full of stories brimming with emotion: a man feels anger and shoots someone; a couple feels lust and commits adultery; a teenager feels despair and commits suicide. The world is a very emotional place.

But not only is the world an emotional place, we are also emotional people. Ultimately that is why the world is an emotional place. The only way to view people is holistically. We are a mixture of body and soul, mind and heart. As much as we would perhaps like to, we don't experience the world in a purely rational way or in a purely emotional way. Neither do we experience other people in a purely rational way or in a purely emotional way. Our experience of the world is a living combination of rational and emotional elements.

This dynamic between mind and emotion is acknowledged in Scripture. For example, the Apostle Paul makes it very clear that how we think will affect how we act. So he tells the Ephesians that 'they must no longer live as the Gentiles do in the futility of their thinking' (Eph. 4:17); and then goes on to show that the path of sanctification and godliness will involve being 'made new in the attitude of your minds' and then putting on the new self (Eph. 4:23, 24).

But not only does our thinking affect our actions, our emotions do as well. For this reason in the following verses Paul counsels the Ephesians that in their anger they should not sin (Eph. 4:26). Another place where this dynamic is seen is in the statement of what Jesus considered was the greatest commandment, 'to love the Lord your God with all your heart and with all your soul and with all your mind and with all your strength' (Mark 12:30). It is not enough to love the Lord with just our minds, because we are not purely rational. We must love him with our heart as well.

Since the world is an emotional place, and we are emotional people, it is hardly surprising to find that the Bible is an emotional book. After all, the Bible is an account of God's acts through people in the world. God's Word doesn't just convey his truth to us in a purely rational way. Rather, it does so in a way that engages our emotions as well, because as previously stated, that truth is contextualized in relationship. It needs to be noted the Psalms are not the only part of Scripture that is full of emotional content – all of it is! The account of creation is not just telling us how God brought the world into being; it is also inviting us to share in the excitement of that event, to wonder at the possibility of life, without sin, in the presence of God. When you move into the later parts of the Pentateuch you are confronted by the law, which on the surface seems very unemotional. However, this is not the case. The law confronts us with the goodness of God and the seriousness of sin. It causes us to feel the shame of failure and the fear of wrath. In the historical books such as Judges we see the relief that accompanies the rise of a saviour, and the anarchy that results when sin is allowed to go unchecked and every man does what he considers to be right. Psalms shows us praise soaring, as some aspect of God's character comes into view, but also the darkness of doubt and depression that so easily overcomes us in this world. The prophets are strident in their denunciation of sin, but in that denunciation they frequently picture God as the wounded party whose faithfulness has been trampled on by an unfaithful partner. On the other hand, they make clear that God's faithfulness and love will not be defeated by mankind's sinfulness. Love always triumphs. Hope's candle is never put out. And the New Testament calls upon us to submit to the rule of God's King, Jesus. He fulfills all of God's promises and in him the rule of God begins to take possession of the world again. Unless we engage the Scriptures at an emotional level, recognising their emotional content, we cannot understand their meaning or feel their force![5]

---

[5] This whole area of feeling the message of the Bible is one that is receiving some attention from scholars at the moment in the area of reader response literary criticism. Recently, Peter Bolt wrote an article in *The Reformed Theological Review* 60 (2001), 1-17. entitled 'Feeling the Cross: Mark's Message of Atonement'.

Peter Bolt argues in that article that Mark's Gospel is structured and written in a way that makes us feel what is going on at the Cross. Through the course of the Gospel the reader is drawn into sympathy with Jesus. Jesus' opponents are relentless in their quest to kill him, a man who through the course of the gospel has only done good. Jesus' friends even

Fourthly, we also need to take into account that God is an emotional God. Christian theology has been reserved about speaking of God in this way. Classical statements about God speak of him 'without passions'. This thinking owes more to the influence of Greek philosophy, however, than it does to the teaching of the Bible. For Aristotle God was the 'unmoved mover'. We are to love him, but he is incapable of loving us. The view of the Bible is very different. The Bible pictures God as a trinity and so the essence of his nature is relationship, and the basis of those relationships is love, for God in his very nature loves (1 John 4:16). It is not at all surprising therefore that the Bible constantly uses emotive language to describe God's relationship with his people:

- He is jealous for his people's love (Exod. 20:5)
- 'He is gracious and compassionate; slow to anger and abounding in love and faithfulness, maintaining love to thousands and forgiving wickedness and rebellion. Yet he does not leave the sin of the guilty unpunished.' (Exod. 34: 6-7)
- He is a husband to his people (Isa. 54:5)

---

betray him. Judas hands him over to the authorities, Peter denies him. His cry of dereliction suggests that even his Father abandons him.

But we don't just feel sympathy for Jesus; we are also distanced from him. The crowd, for example, has been positively characterised, and yet at the last minute they are implicated in his death (15:15). Peter and the disciples are characters the reader has followed from the beginning, we hear their cries of loyalty, but then are witnesses to their fall, and in their fall we see our own fall.

Bolt argues that the portrayal of Jesus' opponents also serves to increase our distance. From the moment of his arrest, Jesus is given over to his opponents, and his friends stand off at a distance. At the end of the account, even his body has to be requested back from Pilate before it can be given to the reader. The opponents are in control. The reader is forced to stand at a distance and watch.

Mark wants us to feel sympathy for Jesus, to be attracted to him, and yet to also feel distanced from him. To feel implicated in his death, which of course we are. But along with all of that is the assurance from the narrative that Jesus came for sinners and that his death is a ransom for lives. As we read the gospel we are not just given a lot of rational information, we are also drawn into the narrative so that we feel what is going on.

- He acts towards his people as a tender father stooping to help them (Hosea 11:1-4)
- Jesus made a whip and cleared the temple as zeal for his father's house consumed him (John 2:13-22)
- This same Jesus wept at the grave of his friend Lazarus (John 11:35)

As a result of these four considerations: the fact that the world is an emotional place, we are emotional people, the Bible is an emotional book and God is an emotional God, it is imperative that we pay heed to the emotional content of the Bible's record. Indeed, I don't believe it is going too far to say that failure to deal with the emotional aspect of the text is a failure to properly exegete and understand the message of the text itself. For example, it is almost impossible to understand the just punishment of Israel unless we feel the betrayal God feels as his beloved people go off and worship other gods. All of this leads to the question of how? How do we tap into the Bible's emotion?

Tapping into the Bible's emotion
In seeking to answer this question R. C. Sproul has some helpful comments that point us in the right direction. Sproul says:

> Preaching calls forth an emotional response. It is not merely an exercise in the transfer of information. The pulpit is the setting for drama. The gospel itself is dramatic. We are not speaking of the sense of drama as a contrived performance or as a make-believe world of play-acting. We are speaking of dramatic truth, truth that shatters the soul, that brings healing and sends the human spirit soaring. It must grieve the Holy Spirit when the dramatic word is recited dispassionately. The preacher doesn't make the gospel dramatic – it already is. To communicate the gospel dramatically is to fit the preaching with the content. Dispassionate preaching is a lie. It denies the content it conveys.[6]

---

[6] R. C. Sproul 'The Whole Man' in *Preaching,* ed. Samuel T. Logan, Evangelical Press, 1986, p 113.

Sproul is making the point that in order to accurately teach the Bible we need to tap into its feeling, or its drama. That is not to say of course, that the traditional task of exegesis is any less important, or should be shortcut. We still need to determine the natural length of a preaching unit, and study it using all the tools we have at our disposal (language, concordances, dictionaries, commentaries, background books and so on).

But now we need to add an extra strand to our preparation, by tapping into the emotion, the feeling, the drama of the passage. In what follows I am going to offer some suggestions about how to do this, illustrating it with reference to Daniel 10–12.

Some helpful suggestions:

(i) Start looking for the emotion and feeling in a passage. This needs to be included as a step in our exegesis of the passage. Often we don't find that level of the text, simply because we are not looking for it. We're too busy tapping into the argument or the flow of thought of a passage to notice the emotion or drama behind that flow of thought. A good way of finding the emotion, or dramatic high point, or mood of a passage is to simply read it aloud slowly and imaginatively asking some of the following questions:

- What is the dramatic high point?
- What emotion is present in the passage?
- What was the writer feeling when he wrote this?
- What did the writer want the readers to feel?

Using these questions let's look at Daniel 10. The passage opens with Daniel receiving a vision. The place and timing of the vision is significant. It is the third year of Cyrus' reign and Daniel is on the banks of the River Tigris. The exiles have returned but Daniel has not! Considering his passionate prayer in Chapter 9, that the exile might come to an end, it is not hard to imagine Daniel's profound disappointment and questioning. Why has God passed over him? Will he miss out on the return altogether? We can imagine him dreaming, longing for life in the land. The vision that comes to him, however, functions at one level as an encouragement to him. It is a vision about conflict. Many of the details of the vision have been described previously in Chapter 8, but they highlight, in this context, that life in the land may not be all that Daniel dreams it is. Greece will overcome Persia, it will then split up into two dynasties and Israel will be caught in the middle of the feuding that goes on between them. In that situation the people in the land must resist, which is exactly the same thing Daniel has had to do in exile. The big message of this vision is that life in the land is not all that different to life in exile. But still the question persists, has Daniel missed out on the return? The answer lies in Chapter 12. In the Old Testament the return from exile is pictured as resurrection. The nation died in exile but rose to new life in the return. In Chapter 12 Daniel is told that although he may have missed out on the dress rehearsal, he has not missed out on the real thing. He will be among the wise that rise to shine like the brightness of the heavens (Dan. 12:3); he will sleep, but rise to receive his inheritance. Not his inheritance in the land, but his inheritance in the kingdom of God! (Dan. 12:13) The narrative is full of emotion when you go looking for it. It includes longing, disappointment and questioning, as well as relief and joy! It is important to discover these moods of the passage if it is to be understood correctly.

(ii) Seek to convey the emotional mood of the passage when preaching it. It is at this point that exegesis meets preaching technique. It is not enough to identify the emotional content of a passage; we must be in sympathy with it as we preach it. Truth that compels is embodied truth. It was so in Jesus' life, 'the word became flesh'; it must be so in our lives and communication as well. Of course this is not an easy thing to do. But for the sake of effective, honest and accurate communication of God's Word we need to seek to pray and think and imagine ourselves into sympathy with the text.

With reference to Daniel again, in order to feel how Daniel must have felt, we must try and put ourselves in his position. How would he have felt as he prayed that the exile might come to an end? Was his dominant desire to escape the pagan culture of Babylon or did he just want to go home? How would he have felt as he saw the exiles return home, but he did not?

As we question the text in this way, we will begin to feel the anguish, heartache, impatience and comfort – then we will be in a position to convey these moods as we communicate.

(iii) Engage the audience emotionally in the introduction. Every preacher knows the importance of those opening few minutes of a talk. People are listening then to determine if they will keep listening! They want to know if what you say will impact them where they are in their lives; if it will help them to cope with the daily grind of life in a fallen world. The introduction, therefore, is the perfect time to tap into the emotion and drama of the passage, and will also be a great help in setting the appropriate mood of the passage under consideration.

In Daniel 10–12, as I analyse the passage, it seems to me that the dominant emotion Daniel was feeling was longing. He desired to depart the pagan culture of Babylon, of exile, and go home. Home is where his heart is. It is where he can stop struggling against Babylonian paganism and worship God in freedom, as the law instructs him to. It is where his inheritance, his land is. It is most likely where he would like to be buried. Once you have identified the dominant emotion you are then in a position to introduce that emotion into the introduction. When I preached on this passage, I started with a quotation from the Indian writer Salmon Rushdie who said, 'Exile is a dream of glorious return'. That quotation aptly captures the mood of Daniel as he wrote these chapters, and sets the tone of the sermon in a way that is sympathetic with the passage itself.

My contention in this chapter has been a simple one. It is that the emotional content, or mood of a passage, needs to be understood if the passage itself is to be understood. For too long we have neglected the emotional level of the text. Rather than regarding emotions as being misleading and manipulative, we need to see them as one of the many layers of the text that needs to be dealt with if we are to properly understand God's Word to us. And armed with that conviction we must look for the emotional content of a passage, and use it to faithfully and forcefully speak God's truth.

SECTION 3

SPECIAL EVENTS

10.

PREACHING AT A WEDDING OR FUNERAL

SIMON MANCHESTER

Most Christians would be glad to have a hundred non-Christians (or more) turn up for an evangelistic talk. The wedding or funeral provides such an opportunity and it should be used well. Of course there are major differences between an evangelistic event and a wedding or funeral, but if the Word of God is to be preached at these 'special events in life', it should be done carefully and helpfully. Often Christian relatives know that this is the only opportunity their friends and family will have to hear the Christian message. Whether or not my own attempts have brought about much fruit, our job is to send out a faithful and engaging message.

The wedding
In my experience this is the most difficult of the 'hatch, match and despatch' events. There is little gratitude (as in the case of a child's dedication or baptism) and there is little humility (as in the case of a funeral). Many of the people are in the prime of life and may well come to the wedding dressed to impress and with a few drinks under the belt already.

Often the couple are re-marrying or have been living together so that everyone comes with a sense that God's ways don't matter much anyway – here may be a couple who are refusing God's will but, nonetheless, the old minister is doing exactly what they want. (There are Christian weddings that are reverent and delightful but it's worth being ready for anything.)

Also the couple have probably been 'co-operative' until now with marriage interviews, preparation classes and even church attendance. So should you preach to help their marriage, gospel them one more time or reach this new crowd that have come for the occasion? The answer to this will probably vary but my own priority is to reach the crowd that has gathered. If we are to 'be prepared in season and out of season' (2 Tim. 4:2), surely this is a responsibility that shouldn't be ignored. The occasion may demand some interest in the marriage issues but with sensitivity this can be used well for wider application and longer-term effects. You have had your times with the couple and now there is an obligation to care for the people present who may be new and are certainly in need of the gospel. It would be a tragedy to waste this opportunity by saying something that is irrelevant, confusing or off-putting.

It makes sense, if at all possible, to use the passages chosen by the couple for their wedding service. This is not as prohibitive as it sounds as there are ways to avoid preaching solely from 1 Corinthians 13! During your preparatory talks to the couple, ask them to steer away from such familiar verses and show them some good alternatives. Readings like Philippians 2:5-11 (on serving); 1 John 4:7-12 (on loving); narrative like John 2:1-11 (the wedding at Cana); or a parable like Matthew 22:1-14 (the wedding banquet) all make good material for wedding sermons. All Scripture is profitable and with sound preparation provides the 'sword' for great effect.

If you do get pushed into 1 Corinthians 13, it comes as a terrific surprise to the guests to explain that the verses didn't originally go to Corinth for a wedding or to provide inspiring gasps but rather to smack the immature Corinthians around the ears! Their natural unloving (self-loving) behaviour is then a great platform for the solution God provides for us all.

I find it helpful when beginning at a wedding to get the congregation on side; the sermon is pretty well the last thing they came for and they think it only has redeeming value in their ears if it is interesting or funny, etc. Sometimes I explain that everyone tries to say something at a wedding (in the reception queue or on their congratulatory card) but that God has something really worth hearing.

Sometimes I 'defend' the sermon slot by explaining that God is the inventor of marriage and we should pick some lines from his book on this occasion to see what he says (and many here may not know). Sometimes I just tell the people I am going to be very brief but, 'What was in those Bible readings?' Do everything you can to get your wedding crowd with you and staying with you through an important message.

Be faithful to your text. There is no point in using it or abusing it to say what you want it to say, if that's not what it really says. Once you are properly prepared on the meaning of the passage you can stop and consider how to connect this simply and urgently to your listeners. For example, if your reading or text is Philippians 2:5-11, you will need (in a line or two) to explain that the context is some dear Christian friends who are drifting into selfishness – the natural direction for us all.

The pagans who come to weddings have few answers to selfish relationships and it's worth pointing out that Philippians 2:5-11 provides the way to a change of mind and a change of lifestyle that revolutionises those who take Christ seriously.

I'm not pretending here to give you the definitive message of Philippians 2:5-11, simply to point out that the relational bankruptcy in the world is enriched by the gospel and that we should seize the opportunity to point that out.

Apart from the great aims of preaching at a wedding (to honour Christ, explain God's Word, challenge the outsider, feed the insider) we should aim to change our listener's perception about Christianity by showing that God's ways are clear, wise, profound, interesting and available. A tall order, but with some careful preparation and some fresh phrases it can be done.

At a wedding with plenty of outsiders I normally don't exceed ten minutes for the sermon. I would rather have them pleasantly surprised than confirming their worst nightmares about long sermons – but that's a personal decision. Without ignoring the couple or the context of marriage it's a short message for everyone.

The funeral

I heard someone say once that no-one but Jesus knows how to get a funeral right. I'm sure this is true. Recognising the difficulties let me humbly suggest some things that I have found helpful.

It is good to have an outline in your mind for the service that will maximise the truth of the gospel. I try to work with one like this:

Welcome: To express appropriate sadness and yet confidence in the hope Jesus offers.

Scriptures: I now read a collection of Bible phrases to summarise the gospel and establish 'grace not works'. This helps enormously before tributes are given and pagan friends make extravagant claims about the worthiness of the deceased to have won their way to glory.

Hymn: Choose something that is thankful/uplifting and well known (if possible) to ensure the musicians avoid dragging.

Bible readings: Perhaps two readings from family or friends that (again) help the cause of the gospel.

Tributes: Try to allow two at most. If three or four or five people want to speak you can be sure it will be repetitious and exhausting for everybody.

Hymn: This is the place for the 'sadder' hymn and gives opportunity for grief before you speak.

Looking forward: You can see the advantage of separating the 'looking back' tributes with the 'looking forward' message. Everyone needs to go forward from the funeral and it is your opportunity to show the way.

Prayers: Appropriate prayers of thanks, for support and for the readiness of the congregation to face the future.

Hymn: A hymn of hope as the coffin is taken out.

When I meet with the family I use a preparation sheet like this:

1. Name of deceased:
    Known as:

2. Date of birth .... and death ....

3. Immediate family:

4. Time and date of service:

5. Order of service:
    (a) Hymn
    (b) Reading(s)
    (c) Tributes –
        ('Looking back') –
    (d) Hymn
    (e) Message
        ('Looking forward') –
    (f) Prayers
    (g) Hymn

6. Arrangements after service:

7. People invited to ....

8. Other details:
    (a) organist
    (b) flower
    (c) item in service

9. Home address of family:

10. Things to know:

11. Name (and phone) of Funeral Director:

When it comes to the funeral sermon be sensitive to the context. I once took a funeral for an 'underworld' figure and the place was full of total outsiders. It was important to point out (and I did) that, 'We don't pretend here that good people go to heaven. Jesus came for sinners so we are not playing a game here that 'X' was really a good person – he probably wasn't. The question for him (and for you one day) is "Are you forgiven?"'

I also took a funeral for a wonderful young Christian man where the tributes were given by non-Christian friends. They were so gushing in their praise that it made it much harder to preach the gospel. It was as if he was perfect so God was unfair and Jesus was unnecessary. I had to begin by saying that 'Y' was wonderfully brought by God to realise his need of forgiveness. He was good by human standards but he knew he wasn't good by God's perfect standards ...'

(I now ask the family to make sure that those they ask to give tributes aim for 5–7 minutes maximum and don't present a perfect person, which is unrealistic and unhelpful to everyone else.)

Now what to say as you step up for your own 5–10 minutes on 'looking forward'?

Again I have no great successes to tell you about, but we do need to avoid the terrible stereotypes we see on television. This is not the time for pious clichés or professional sentimentality. We have a range of people sitting there from the traumatised to the careless. While everyone knows that something serious has happened, many people have the most amazing ability to resist the Saviour God provides.

I find it helpful to begin with an explanation of what I am doing. 'I'm going to take a few minutes (only) now to talk about the way forward. You and I have to go forward and if we're honest/sensible we'll admit our need for help. What we really need is an expert on the future and God has given us one...', etc. I find this a good thing to stress.

Then to the text and some reasons for the text. 'We don't want my opinion (or anyone's) at this point. We need some guarantee that is bigger than all of us. We don't want some wishful thinking. We need some information that is solid ground to stand on. If you want to know why the Christian is confident about the future it's not because he thinks he's great but because God makes promises – and knows how to keep them'.

We all have some favourite and well-worn passages for a funeral – but keep rethinking them!

For example if you preach from John 11, ask your listeners why verse 25 is more important than verse 43. The words to Lazarus might seem more exciting but they're to one man and offering a resuscitation. The words to Martha are for all people and offering a resurrection. And if Lazarus listened to verse 43 why don't you listen to verse 25...?

If you speak from John 14 you will want to point out that when Jesus said 'I am going ... to prepare a place for you', he didn't mean going straight up but via the cross. And since he prepared the place by dying, why don't you secure your future by trusting in him? If you speak from 1 Corinthians 15, do you realise the original readers were losing their future by various preoccupations with the here and now?

At a very difficult funeral the principle in Deuteronomy 29:29 is good to keep in mind: 'The secret things belong to the Lord our God, but the things revealed belong to us and to our children forever...'. We can say, 'We don't know why this loss has happened. It's a "secret" to everyone but God. On the other hand he has "revealed" some things which are of great comfort and enough for us to know at this point...' and so on.

Whatever your text, get it clear in its context so that you speak with integrity as well as usefulness. Even Deuteronomy 29:29 comes in the context of burning questions for God – just as may be asked at the funeral.

It is always difficult to know what to say when the deceased showed no signs of faith. This is why the two parts of the funeral ('looking back' and 'looking forward') can help. We cannot know where, at their end, people stand spiritually. If salvation comes when a person 'calls on the Lord' (Rom. 10:13) then we have to admit, as J. C. Ryle once said, that there could be many surprises in heaven.

Better to talk to the people in the pews and if necessary say to them, 'This is a message for us. We are the people with an opportunity to listen and respond. 'X' had his own opportunities and we have ours. Let's not judge someone else but decide our own future', and so on.

At the end of the service we will have prayed (because a funeral can be stressful as well as full of opportunity), we will have prepared in a way that honours Christ and provides solid hope, and we will be more conscious than ever that God says, 'heaven and earth will pass away but my words will never pass away' (Mark 13:31).

May his words bring many to life.

11.

SPEAKING ABOUT SENSITIVE ISSUES TO A CHRISTIAN AUDIENCE

DAVID COOK

It is a common way to think that there are certain parts of our lives that are our own business and nothing to do with God. However, we see in the Bible that God directed his people in all personal areas such as sexual ethics, polygamy, family life, how to give birth, circumcision, inheritance, adoption, treatment of a corpse, burial rites, personal hygiene, toilet placement, food preparation, and appropriate foods to eat. All of these laws were evidence that God's Lordship was intrusive, that his interest in his people's welfare was all encompassing.

The central affirmation of Judaism is Deuteronomy 6:4 'Hear O Israel: The LORD our God, the LORD is one'. This is known as the 'Shema' and continues to take a central place today in the Jewish synagogue service. Not only does the *Shema* affirm the unity of God, that he is one, but also that he rules, that he is Lord and that Israel had to recognise the jurisdiction of God's Lordship as unlimited.

Because God's Lordship *is* like this, the speaker will often be speaking about issues from the Bible that secular speakers would consider to be off limits. If God has a mind on these things it is important for us to sensitively, accurately yet clearly state that mind to our fellow Christians.

In this chapter I want to deal with two sensitive issues, sex and money, and look at principles of preparation for a talk on each. Then I will deal with one example of a sensitive political issue.

Speaking about sex

Advertisers, big business, and media owners all know the power of sex to sell their product or lift their ratings. It is impossible to escape the world's alluring message that human sexual expression is animal instinct driven. According to this view sex is natural, the partner is a sex object to be used (and abused if necessary) and then after use may be discarded if it suits one's purpose.

The sex drive is a powerful one and is very destructive when it is uncontrolled. Sex outside its God-intended environment of a lifelong covenant relationship is like throwing petrol on the barbecue, it is dangerous and destructive.

Sex has been designed by God for one environment, marriage, where it builds intimacy and satisfaction. To take it out of that environment is like syphoning petrol from the petrol tank and using it for other than its intended purpose.

God invented sex so we must speak about it from his Word; the world is filling our minds with destructive nonsense making our silence as Christian speakers a guilty silence.

My goal in speaking about sex is to speak so that any grandparents present will want to buy the CD of the talk for their grandchildren to hear. If I can talk in a way that is clear, faithful to the Bible and not offensive to the older generation, then I have achieved my goal.

Here are some do's and don'ts for preparing a talk on sex.

Do's:
- Do speak realistically, so it is quite clear what you are saying.
- Do anticipate the variety of experience of those listening to you. There will be some people who battle with homosexual feelings, recognise their struggles and have a word of encouragement for them. There will be those who have been abused sexually; and others who battle with pornography, you are there not to condemn them

but in recognising their presence to encourage them in sexual purity.

- Do recognise that all of us are called to live in sexual purity whether single, married or once married, so offer solutions that help in the maintenance of purity.
- Do talk about yourself, but only so far as it involves your own standards of maintaining purity.
- Do be positive. God is not anti-sex, but is against the misuses and abuse of this gift.
- Do expound the Bible; you are not there just to give your opinions.

Don'ts:

- Don't use the occasion to get a laugh. Making sex an object of humour, especially in a Christian context, is both pathetic and cheapening.
- Don't be graphic to the point of embarrassment. Don't get involved in mechanical issues or name parts of the anatomy involved.
- Don't use personal case studies; they are confidential, not for public consumption.
- Don't, by what you say, encourage adolescents present to develop an unhealthy interest in experimentation.
- Don't create the impression that there is no sin as great as sexual sin. Read Paul's list in Romans Chapter 1 and you will see that he puts homosexual expression and uncleanness alongside gossipping and disobedience to parents as sins unacceptable to God.
- Don't pontificate as one who is not subject to sexual temptation; be honest about your own frailty.

If you want to be more open in a youth group context it may be helpful to separate people into two groups, men and women. This can open the way to speak more frankly and will facilitate questions.

I try to preach on sex at least once every year as a reminder of God's Lordship even over this area of privacy.

I have given talks on sex from the following texts:

Genesis 1 and 2 – especially Genesis 1:28 'be fruitful and increase'; and Genesis 2:24 'a man will leave his father and mother and be united to his wife and they will become one flesh'.

Proverbs 9 – Lady Wisdom and Madame Folly.

Proverbs 30:1-19 – 'the way of a man with a maiden'.

Song of Solomon.

Matthew 5:27-30 – adultery in the mind is adultery.

1 Corinthians 6:12-20.

1 Corinthians 7 – marriage and singleness.

Ephesians 5:22-23 – marriage.

See the pyramid on the opposite page for preparing a talk on sex from Matthew 5:27-30.

Speaking about money
Money is an integral part of everyday life; therefore what God has to say about it must be carefully considered by us all.

If you are a group leader then don't hesitate to speak about the subject. It is part of your leadership responsibility to remind people to be wise and generous in its use.

My goal in preaching about money is to cause people to be shrewd, strategic and generous in their giving. I don't want to offend people; neither do I want them to be challenged without being changed.

One of the devil's favourite tactics is to allow us to be challenged in hearing the talk and then afterwards to convince us that everything we have just heard is unreal and has little to do with the realities of life in the real world.

The movement of the will to habitual change towards godliness is the goal of the speaker, and in the case of money, godliness is in the shape of generosity.

In speaking about wealth I need to recognise:

- The great pressure on my hearers from family and friends in this area. I have yet to hear of any financial adviser who has advised the client that she or he has enough wealth set aside. (They may need to give that advice; we don't need to heed it.) More money, the best

PREACHING PYRAMID

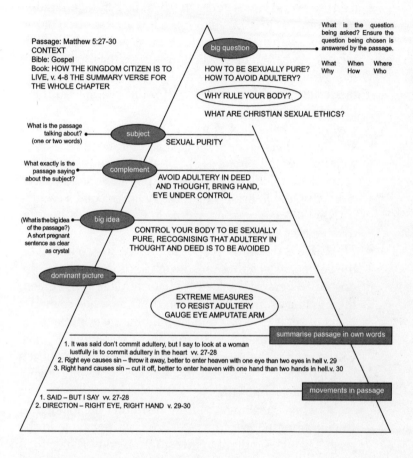

Passage: Matthew 5:27-30
CONTEXT
Bible: Gospel
Book: HOW THE KINGDOM CITIZEN IS TO LIVE, v. 4-8 THE SUMMARY VERSE FOR THE WHOLE CHAPTER

What is the question being asked? Ensure the question being chosen is answered by the passage.

What   When   Where
Why   How   Who

big question

HOW TO BE SEXUALLY PURE?
HOW TO AVOID ADULTERY?

WHY RULE YOUR BODY?

WHAT ARE CHRISTIAN SEXUAL ETHICS?

What is the passage talking about? (one or two words)

subject

SEXUAL PURITY

What exactly is the passage saying about the subject?

complement

AVOID ADULTERY IN DEED AND THOUGHT, BRING HAND, EYE UNDER CONTROL

(What is the big idea of the passage?) A short pregnant sentence as clear as crystal

big idea

CONTROL YOUR BODY TO BE SEXUALLY PURE, RECOGNISING THAT ADULTERY IN THOUGHT AND DEED IS TO BE AVOIDED

dominant picture

EXTREME MEASURES TO RESIST ADULTERY GAUGE EYE AMPUTATE ARM

1. It was said don't commit adultery, but I say to look at a woman lustfully is to commit adultery in the heart vv. 27-28
2. Right eye causes sin – throw it away, better to enter heaven with one eye than two eyes in hell v. 29
3. Right hand causes sin – cut it off, better to enter heaven with one hand than two hands in hell.v. 30

summarise passage in own words

1. SAID – BUT I SAY vv. 27-28
2. DIRECTION – RIGHT EYE, RIGHT HAND v. 29-30

movements in passage

Application: (What does it tell us about?)

GOD: *Interested in the purity of his people's sex life. Honours the marriage covenant. Takes adultery seriously.*

US: *We lust. We must take radical steps to preserve purity.*

Necessary – (Always necessary for all people) *Be careful to resist adultery in all its forms.*

Possible – (Sometimes possible for some people) *Avoid places where temptation is prominent e.g. newsagent, barber shop*

Impossible – (How the passage cannot be applied) *A disciple of Christ sees sex as a self indulgent toy to be indulged indiscriminately.*

117

stocks, another investment property is all part of the pressure on us in the quest for security.

- The pre-World War II generation was largely a generation of tithers. In their misunderstanding of the place of the law in the Christian's life they gave one tenth of their income away. We understand much better the reality of living under grace, not law, and yet grace very often gets much less out of us than the 10% the law got from the previous generation.

- Giving is a habit that is never convenient; whether you are a university student on government benefits, newly-weds saving for a house deposit, new parents saving for school fees, middle-aged consolidating superannuation or elderly on the pension – generosity never comes easily.

  Now, not at some better time in the future, is the time to develop generous giving habits.

- The Bible is the source of our authority, so expound it on the subject of wealth. Don't divorce exhortation from the gospel. When Paul urges the Corinthians to complete their giving as promised (2 Cor. 8:11), he does so on the basis of what God has done for them. 2 Corinthians 8:9 provides the gospel basis for the exhortation, 'Jesus Christ, rich as he was became poor by choice to enrich you by grace'. Therefore follow his example of giving and complete your gift.

  So when speaking about money don't be apologetic. Encouraging people to be generous in response to the gospel is inviting them to invest for eternity (Luke 16:9) and that is a privilege.

- The need to be careful not to be legalistic regarding the lifestyle of other believers. Can a person trust in Christ and buy shares, have a mortgage, drive a BMW? Of course they can, your role is not to lay down rules and regulations for others, but rather to teach the gospel, urge generosity and point out the dangers of wealth.

  Remember that wealth is a very good servant but a demanding and tyrannical master.

I have given talks on money from the following texts:

Psalm 24 – God created the earth therefore he owns it. We are not owners but managers of it.

Genesis 1:28 – the basis of our management and rule of God's creation is this Word from the Creator.

Deuteronomy 26 – God's ownership recognised through the tithe.

The book of Proverbs on the theme of wealth – 10:15; 10:22; 11:4; 13:7; 18:11; 23:5; 28:20.

Ecclesiastes 5:8ff – wealth adds to the meaninglessness of life.

Matthew 6:1-4 – acts of generosity for public reward.

Luke 12:13-21 – the importance of being rich towards God.

Luke 16:1-15 – the need to use wealth wisely.

Luke 16:19-31 – a man who used wealth foolishly.

Acts 4:32-37 – the generosity of the church.

1 Corinthians 16:1-4 – the early church's habit of giving.

2 Corinthians 8 and 9 – Paul's exhortation to be generous.

1 Timothy 6:3-21 – the warnings regarding wealth.

See the pyramid on the next page for preparing a talk on money from Luke 16:1-15.

Speaking on sensitive issues

How should a speaker deal with having to prepare a talk on a sensitive political issue?

A few years back a very 'hot' issue in Australia was the debate regarding our involvement in the 'coalition of the willing' against Saddam Hussein in Iraq. As far as I could tell the nation was divided about 60%–40% on this issue, against our involvement.

In situations like that these are the principles we need to keep in mind:

- I am not giving this talk to push my own opinions. As a Christian speaker my concern is to bring the mind of God (the Bible) to bear on a complex political issue.

119

PREACHING PYRAMID

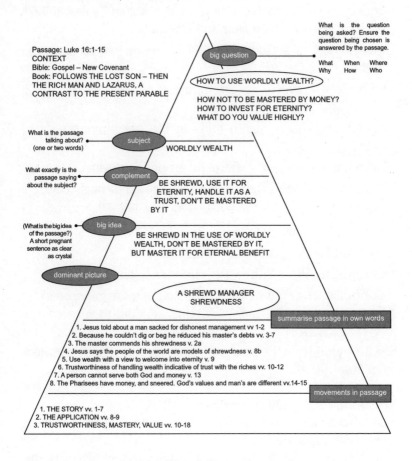

Passage: Luke 16:1-15
CONTEXT
Bible: Gospel – New Covenant
Book: FOLLOWS THE LOST SON – THEN
THE RICH MAN AND LAZARUS, A
CONTRAST TO THE PRESENT PARABLE

big question

What is the question being asked? Ensure the question being chosen is answered by the passage.

What   When   Where
Why   How   Who

HOW TO USE WORLDLY WEALTH?

HOW NOT TO BE MASTERED BY MONEY?
HOW TO INVEST FOR ETERNITY?
WHAT DO YOU VALUE HIGHLY?

What is the passage talking about? (one or two words)

subject

WORLDLY WEALTH

What exactly is the passage saying about the subject?

complement

BE SHREWD, USE IT FOR
ETERNITY, HANDLE IT AS A
TRUST, DON'T BE MASTERED
BY IT

(What is the big idea of the passage?) A short pregnant sentence as clear as crystal

big idea

BE SHREWD IN THE USE OF WORLDLY
WEALTH, DON'T BE MASTERED BY IT,
BUT MASTER IT FOR ETERNAL BENEFIT

dominant picture

A SHREWD MANAGER
SHREWDNESS

summarise passage in own words

1. Jesus told about a man sacked for dishonest management vv 1-2
2. Because he couldn't dig or beg he reduced his master's debts vv. 3-7
3. The master commends his shrewdness v. 2a
4. Jesus says the people of the world are models of shrewdness. v. 8b
5. Use wealth with a view to welcome into eternity v. 9
6. Trustworthiness of handling wealth indicative of trust with the riches vv. 10-12
7. A person cannot serve both God and money v. 13
8. The Pharisees have money, and sneered. God's values and man's are different vv.14-15

movements in passage

1. THE STORY vv. 1-7
2. THE APPLICATION vv. 8-9
3. TRUSTWORTHINESS, MASTERY, VALUE vv. 10-18

Application: (What does it tell us about?)

GOD: *Values shrewdness (Matt. 10-16). Is eternal. Rules as Lord. Values differently to us.*

US: *Can be dishonest, called to be shrewd, trustworthy, not to be mastered by wealth but by God. Value differently to God.*

Necessary – (Always necessary for all people) *Be shrewd and use wealth to invest for eternity (not like the man of vv. 19-31)*

Possible – (Sometimes possible for some people) *People are eternal, to invest for welcome in eternity is to invest in the eternal welfare of people.*

Impossible – (How the passage cannot be applied) *Hoard wealth. Invest in that which pays dividends for this life. Values wealth over people. Be careless, sloppy, foolish in dealing with money.*

- The Bible has no direct word on such issues; therefore I need to come with the correct questions for it to answer. My question will not be: Should our nation be at war with Iraq? But, should our nation be involved in a just war and what is a just war?
- I will try to keep as open a political mind as possible. For example, if I am going to be critical of political groups, I will try to be evenly critical or equally praising of all groups. I want to avoid the charge of political bias as much as that is possible and the reality is that there are matters to be critical of and commend in all parties.
- Politics is dangerous ground because it is a divisive and sensitive issue! Yet we believe that just as God's Lordship intrudes into all areas of life, so as a citizen of God's Kingdom I am to bring his mind to bear on political matters.
- The Christian must not simply swallow the argument that the church should be kept separate (and silent) from the state. Just as all other citizens have the freedom to express and impress their view, so the Christian has that same freedom, indeed we believe we speak the very mind of God as we speak the Bible into the secular situation.
- At the heart of our creed, which we regularly pray is, 'Your will be done on earth as it is in heaven'.
- Never personalise the issue, this may mean never naming a political party or politician. The reason is that once the politician or group is named, the Bible is no longer heard. Politics is one of those areas where even the most biblically literate believers are apt not to allow the Bible to critique their fundamental assumptions about politics.

  The social justice of the left may mean we tend to give them the benefit of the doubt in every issue. Similarly the conservative ethical position of the right means we may tend to give them the benefit of the doubt in every issue.
- Application is a big issue when dealing with ethical-political issues. Your talk may be of help to people with

their thinking and move them towards a change of mind.

Sometimes you will want to move people to action as well.

Please refer to the pyramid and note the three levels of application. Under the 'necessary' I can show people how the passage should apply to all people at all times.

Under the 'possible' I can suggest ways of responding to the issue – these are suggestions and may or may not apply to everyone in the group; it is here that I will suggest options for action.

Under the 'impossible' I will show how the passage cannot possibly apply.

- When dealing with a subject like this, you will need to give people an opportunity to ask further questions. Options for this could include a special mid-week Bible study combining all the study cell groups into one larger group.

An outline of such a study follows: 'Christians and war – do we fight?'

See the pyramid on the opposite page for preparing a talk on Romans 13:1-7.

Christians and war – do we fight?
Stephen Young, St Thomas' Anglican Church, North Sydney – 2003

BRAIN TEASERS:

On Violence...
Would you be justified in taking violent action in the following situations?

a) You come across a youth assaulting an old lady on the street.
b) You catch a burglar hanging out of your window with your new DVD player in hand.
c) You are a member of the police and spot a burglar hanging out of a window with a DVD player in hand.
d) You make a fair tackle while playing football and the person gets up and punches you.

PREACHING PYRAMID

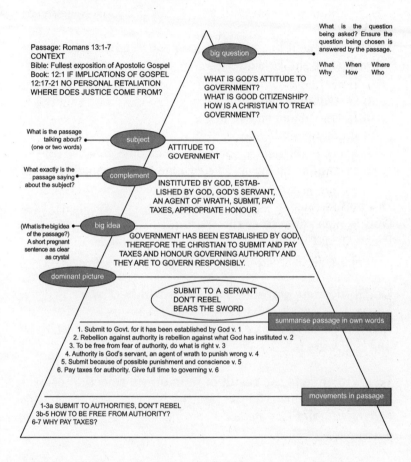

What is the question being asked? Ensure the question being chosen is answered by the passage.

What   When   Where
Why   How   Who

Passage: Romans 13:1-7
CONTEXT
Bible: Fullest exposition of Apostolic Gospel
Book: 12:1 IF IMPLICATIONS OF GOSPEL
12:17-21 NO PERSONAL RETALIATION
WHERE DOES JUSTICE COME FROM?

big question

WHAT IS GOD'S ATTITUDE TO GOVERNMENT?
WHAT IS GOOD CITIZENSHIP?
HOW IS A CHRISTIAN TO TREAT GOVERNMENT?

What is the passage talking about? (one or two words)

subject

ATTITUDE TO GOVERNMENT

What exactly is the passage saying about the subject?

complement

INSTITUTED BY GOD, ESTAB-LISHED BY GOD, GOD'S SERVANT, AN AGENT OF WRATH, SUBMIT, PAY TAXES, APPROPRIATE HONOUR

(What is the big idea of the passage?) A short pregnant sentence as clear as crystal

big idea

GOVERNMENT HAS BEEN ESTABLISHED BY GOD, THEREFORE THE CHRISTIAN TO SUBMIT AND PAY TAXES AND HONOUR GOVERNING AUTHORITY AND THEY ARE TO GOVERN RESPONSIBLY.

dominant picture

SUBMIT TO A SERVANT
DON'T REBEL
BEARS THE SWORD

summarise passage in own words

1. Submit to Govt. for it has been established by God v. 1
2. Rebellion against authority is rebellion against what God has instituted v. 2
3. To be free from fear of authority, do what is right v. 3
4. Authority is God's servant, an agent of wrath to punish wrong v. 4
5. Submit because of possible punishment and conscience v. 5
6. Pay taxes for authority. Give full time to governing v. 6

movements in passage

1-3a SUBMIT TO AUTHORITIES, DON'T REBEL
3b-5 HOW TO BE FREE FROM AUTHORITY?
6-7 WHY PAY TAXES?

Application: (What does it tell us about?)

GOD: *Establishes, institutes authority. Authority serves him. Authority agents of his wrath.*
         God of good order.

US: *Need order, rule. Can rebel but should submit to order.*

Necessary – (Always necessary for all people) *submit, respect Government, pay taxes.*

Possible – (Sometimes possible for some people) B*e honest, respect political leaders.*

Impossible – (How the passage cannot be applied) *Subversion against legitimate Government. What about unjust rule?*

e) You are a soldier in war and have an enemy soldier in your sights as he eats his lunch.

On War...

The Government has re-introduced conscription and you are called up to fight. Do you

a) Go willingly and fight,
b) Refuse to join and go to gaol,
c) Run away and hide,
d) Serve in the military but request a non-combative role, or
e) Pretend to be insane at your medical examination.

Biblical Issues
God is sovereign over the nations
Isaiah 40:15-17; Daniel 1:1-2; Daniel 4:17, 34-35
Nothing has ever happened – or will happen – outside God's control.

God's ultimate purpose for this world is peace
Micah 4:1-4; Isaiah 9:6-8; Revelation 21:3-4
No godly person can love war and violence. It is always terrible and God hates it.

War/Violence is the result of humanity's rejection of God
Genesis 3-4; Romans 3:9-18; James 4:1-2
Our rejection of God makes us violent and cruel towards each other.

Read Romans 12:17-13:7
How can Romans 12:17-21 be reconciled with Romans 13:4?
What is the purpose of government?
What should our attitude be to our government?

The Bible is not a pacifist book
Exodus 20:13; Matthew 5:38-39, 43-45; Romans 12:17-21 – *misapplied!*
Ecclesiastes 3:8; Luke 3:14; 7:1-10; Acts 10:1-8; Luke 14:31-32
Early church and post-reformation pacifism. Pacifism is naïve about human depravity and misunderstands the Bible.

Rulers bear the sword as God's agents of justice in this world

2 Chronicles 19:5-7; Psalm 82:2-4; Romans 13:3-4; 1 Peter 2:13-14

'Just war' tradition...

Those in government have a responsibility to promote peace and justice in this world – including by means of force.

Christians must submit to and pray for our government

Romans 13:1-2,5; 1 Peter 2:13-19; 1 Timothy 2:1-4; Luke 20:25; 1 Samuel 24:6-7, 26:9-11; Jeremiah 27:5-8; 29:7; Luke 23:1-4; Acts 24:5, 17-21; Acts 5:29; Daniel 3, 6

Early church loyalty to Rome...

Even if we disagree with the government (or it is unjust), we must not break the law or undermine its rule (except privately giving precedence to God's law).

We must pray and supportively encourage the government to rule for justice and peace.

We must encourage the military to do likewise and not blame them for doing so.

There is no justification in the Bible for 'holy war'

Deuteronomy 20, Joshua, Matthew 26:47-56; John 18:36; Ephesians 6:12

Crusades, post-Reformation religious wars...

God's agenda is not worldly – his kingdom is a spiritual, heavenly kingdom. We cannot claim a divine mandate for earthly wars.

War is a sign of the times

Mark 13:5-8; Revelation 6:1-11

Repent, hold on, take heart and testify!

There is peace available now

Romans 5:1; Philippians 4:6; Ephesians 2:14-18

The peace (with God and others) which begins now and lasts forever is available in Jesus Christ.

Conclusions

For the war-monger – repent!

For the pacifist – right on, but wise up!

For the sceptic – submit!

For the welcomer – be careful!
For the undecided – pray!

1. Is it right for Christians who disagree with this war on Iraq to protest? Why/why not?
2. Why should Christians work for peace in this world (if at all)?
3. Under what conditions (if any) should a nation go to war?

Biblical issues applied: just war theory and the invasion of Iraq

Warning: 'The Bible was not written to governments about when to go to war – but to God's people about how to live in this war-ridden world.' (Dean Phillip Jensen, Sydney, 2003)

Nevertheless...

In a fallen world, rulers will sometimes have to go to war for 'the object of securing peace, of punishing evil-doers, and of uplifting the good' (Augustine).

1. Is there just cause?
2. Is the intention to restore justice/peace/the common good?
3. Is the action a last resort?
4. Is it instigated by the highest government authority?
5. Are the goals limited?
6. Is the force used proportional to the threat?
7. Will there be minimal casualties, especially amongst non-combatants?
8. When contemplating an offensive war, is there a reasonable hope of success?

PRAYER: for peaceful and quiet lives for sharing the gospel (1 Tim. 2:1-4); for minimal suffering; for wise and upright leadership; that others will turn to God in these last days and find true peace with God.

12.

CHILDREN'S TALKS

SANDY GALEA

I once gave a series of talks on the book of Jonah to eighty children aged between eight and twelve years. As the week progressed I gave the children the opportunity to write down questions they'd like answered. Here are a few of the questions the children asked:

- If God created the heavens and the earth, does that mean he created hell?
- If God said we should love everyone even our enemies then should we love Satan?
- If Jesus is God and God is the Holy Spirit and they are one – when Jesus died wouldn't that mean there (sic) be no God around because they are one?
- When Jesus died on the cross to forgive everyone's sins how can he forgive mine before I'm alive?
- Why didn't God create everyone to believe in him?
- Who do we pray to? God? Jesus?
- Does God hate?
- Why did God make pain?
- Why did Satan go bad?
- Can heaven get full?

I rang my husband a couple of times that week to ask his advice on how to handle some of the questions. At one point he stopped and asked, 'How old are these children?'

The problem was not that they were asking questions – it's a thrill to see children wrestling with God's Word. The challenge was how to answer their questions in ways that would help them grow in their understanding. To take huge concepts like God's justice, predestination and the nature of the trinity, and explain them in ways that are helpful for children.

Far too often in our churches those who teach the children are the young – young in age and/or young in faith. As a result they are often ill-equipped to teach children the truths of Scripture or to handle children's questions.

So who should teach our children?

Children's workers in our churches must be Christian. Unfortunately sometimes even this is compromised at the expense of filling the gap in the teaching programme. Not only should they be thoroughly converted, but they should be maturing in their faith. What is the point of having someone who is a gifted communicator but a poor role model? Immature Christians should not teach children. Children learn not only from what we say, but by the very lives we live. Maturity must come before giftedness.

Not only should children's workers be growing in godliness, but they should be growing in their understanding of the Bible. Our children's workers should know where in the Bible to find answers to the questions such as, does God hate, why did God make pain, why did Satan go bad?

So what does the Bible say in answering these questions? And how would you tailor your answer to a child?

If you want to become good at giving effective children's talks then you will need to be:

a) *Prayerful* – We must begin and end with prayer. This is God's work, not our work. Express your absolute dependence on him by bringing both your preparation and your children before him.

b) *Persistent* – The first children's talk I did was in 1985. I think I was asked to do it because I was a trained teacher. Being a teacher is no guarantee of success, as I soon found out. When it was all over I said to my husband, 'I'm never ever going to do one of those again!' And I didn't – for six years. When I did try again it took me at least a year of giving a children's talk every week before I began to feel confident.

c) *Teachable* – It is essential that you are able to listen and change as a result of feedback. It is the only way to improve. The most painful way of receiving feedback is to actually watch yourself. We record on video many of the children's talks done at church, and then we come together as a group and watch. It is a painful but extremely helpful process. There is nothing like watching yourself on video to motivate you to improve.

d) *Resourceful* – You need to be able to adapt ideas or stories that you come across. I have an 'Ideas Folder'. Some of the ideas which go into this folder remain there for years before I have an opportunity to use them. If I'd left it up to my memory those ideas would have been lost forever.

The ideal would be to have a team of people praying together, working together, brainstorming together and giving each other feedback on a regular basis.

God promises that his Word will always do its work. When God's Word goes out, lives are changed – little lives are changed.

Unfortunately, sometimes, how we teach our children gets in the way of what we teach them. Children's talks function in the same way for children as sermons do for adults. And sometimes our talks are long, complicated, predictable and irrelevant. Poor children's talks tend to leave the children numb to the Word of God; their glazed looks tell it all. The Bible is not boring. It is anything but boring. Rather, it is our mishandling of it that is the problem.

Poor children's talks come in many different shapes and sizes, examples of which can include the following:

- Teaching the Bible as a list of 'do's' and 'don'ts'. Moralizing the Bible;

- Too long (often because we haven't put the time or effort into preparing it);
- Too complicated, either because it's a three point children's talk, or because the words are too big and the sentences too long; and
- Forcing a good illustration we've found to fit the passage, whether it actually does or not.

On the other hand a good children's talk will be clear, concrete and creative.

1. Be clear
A poor children's talk tries to do too much. If you aim for more you will always get less.

Each talk should have one clearly stated point. This point needs to be clearly stated in one short sentence or phrase. For example:

'Listen to Jesus' (*Mary and Martha*, Luke 10:38-42)
'Jesus is God's Son and we must obey him' (*Calming of the Storm*, Mark 4:35-41)

This is very hard to do in practice, as we often want to qualify our points. For example, if you are teaching 'predestination' (God chooses some but not all) you may be tempted to qualify and say, 'but God calls all people everywhere to repent' (human choice and responsibility). This is where keeping the big picture in view is very important. A diet of solid biblical teaching week after week will give the children all the important truths God wants them to hang onto. Don't try to give them all the truths in one session or even try to teach them a couple of truths in one session.

One talk = one point.

The language we use must be carefully chosen. When I first began to write children's talks, I spent some time looking at the language of quality children's literature (for example, Picture Books of the Year). I noticed the following:

(i) *The language is simple.* There are no 'big' words. Not only are the words not 'big' – but few words are used to tell the story. Every word is carefully chosen. There are no unnecessary words. The story is therefore simple and uncluttered.

(ii) *Words and pictures work together to tell the story.* The words don't have to tell the entire story. The pictures (the visual clues) tell that part of the story which the words leave out. This principle can be applied to children's talks. In the talk 'Obey Jesus = Obey Mum and Dad'[1], Johnny is questioned by his Mum about a missing ten dollar note. No words are spoken, but Johnny's visual clues (he turns slightly to one side, pulls out a ten dollar note, looks at it and shoves it back in his pocket) tell the unspoken part of the story.

(iii) *Short sentences.* Children's books have short (sometimes very short) sentences. Here are the first three lines of a talk I wrote on John 10:[2]

Once there lived a shepherd.
He was a good shepherd.
He had lots of sheep.

As adults we would probably say in one sentence, 'There once lived a good shepherd who had lots of sheep'. Breaking it up helps children to take in the information in small chunks. This helps to make the story clear to them.

(iv) *Repetition.* Picture books are full of it. Why? Because children love the sound of it, and they love to say it. Repetition also helps children to remember. When writing your talk, look for repetition.

For example: Genesis 1

---

[1] S. Galea, *Children's Talks - A Practical Guide,* SMBC Press, Sydney, 2000, p 89.
[2] ibid. 'The Good Shepherd' pp 55, 57.

'And God said,
"Let there be...
and there was...
and it was good.
There was evening and morning,
Day..."'

2. Be concrete

The Bible is full of abstract truths. Salvation, holiness, grace, repentance, faith... are all abstract concepts. Children are concrete thinkers.

I once heard about a talk where an adult was urging the children to give their hearts to the Lord. A little girl, whose grandfather had just been through open heart surgery, went white with fear and leaned over and said to her dad, 'I'm not giving my heart to Jesus!'

If we remain in the abstract our children won't begin to learn until they have reached their early teens.

So how do you take the abstract and move it into the concrete? You tell stories. Stories 'flesh' out the abstract idea. Stories take the abstract and put them into relationship contexts. Therefore, your aim should be to tell a story.

3. Be creative

We need to be engaging. We need to stimulate the child's senses. The best way to engage children is to get them involved in the story.

But how do you involve the children in the story without a long rehearsal prior to each meeting? Below is a list of ways to involve the audience in the telling of the story:

(i) *The audience makes sound effects.*
Example: 'Calming of the Storm'[3] – use the audience to make the sound of the wind and the rain.

(ii) *The audience becomes a character.*
Example: 'The Pirate'[4] – the audience is the Captain's voice.

---

[3] ibid. p. 82.
[4] ibid. p. 77.

(iii) *The audience becomes a group.*
Example: 'David and Goliath'[5] – half the audience becomes the Israelites; the other half becomes the Philistines.
Example: 'Calming of the Storm'[6] – the audience become the disciples in the boat.

(iv) *The audience adds atmosphere.*
Example: 'Trust In Me'[7] – the narrator says, 'Poor Jason' (in a sad and sympathetic tone) every time a person lets Jason down and the audience repeats 'Poor Jason!'
Example: Someone caught stealing, fighting, lying, etc. Audience responds: 'Uh-Oh!'

(v) *The audience says a line on cue; this line is repeated throughout the talk and is the point of the talk.*
Example: 'The Birth of Jesus'[8] – the audience's cue: '...call him Jesus, which means....' The audience responds: 'God saves.'
Example: 'Martha and Mary' – the audience's cue: 'Martha looked around. Where was Mary?' The audience responds: 'Listening to Jesus.'

(vi) *The audience repeats the entire story line by line, action by action.*
Example: 'The Good Shepherd' (Version 2)[9].

What does this involvement do for the child? It helps them to enter into some sort of understanding of how the characters in the story felt and why the characters said or did certain things.

I did the *Calming of the Storm* for a large school assembly a few years ago. The noise the children made when making the sound of the wind and the rain was deafening. On top of

---

[5] ibid. p. 64.
[6] ibid. p. 82.
[7] ibid. p. 60.
[8] ibid. p. 68.
[9] ibid. p. 57.

that was the thunder sound effect. Add to that the movement of six hundred children rocking side to side as they were tossed about in the 'boat'. Darken the hall, add lightning and you've created a very chaotic, very loud storm, which the children are in the middle of. At the end of the assembly a kindergarten child came up to me and said, 'I'm glad that Jesus stopped the storm. I was a little scared!'

If you've ever been caught out on a boat in a storm, the two things that stay in your mind are the continual movement and the noise. The boat and everything in it is tossed about. Nothing stays still. And storms are very, very loud. That's what makes them so frightening.

By creating both the movement and the noise of a storm you allow the children the opportunity to experience a taste of what it was like for the disciples. They were terrified. These experienced fishermen were sure they were going to drown. When Jesus, with a word, makes everything still, everything silent, the children can then understand the disciples' response, 'Who is this man? Even the wind and the waves obey him!'

Research tells us that if we hear something we are likely to remember about 10% of what was said. If we hear and see something we are likely to remember about 50% of it. But if we hear, see and do it we are likely to remember between 80–90%.

We are more likely to remember what is being taught if we participate in the telling of the story, rather than simply hearing the story, or hearing and seeing the story played out for us.

In a series of talks on Jonah, I wrote my longest, most demanding talk ever. In the talk I required the children to be the sailors on the boat with Jonah. As the sailors, they had to load the cargo (large cardboard boxes) on the boat and then off the boat. This became a competitive team game in the middle of the talk. Teams frantically passed the cargo over their heads loading it onto the boat, and later throwing it overboard. They also wore newspaper sailor hats, rocked from side to side, looked terrified and repeated some lines.

Not only were they the sailors but they also had to create the sound of the wind. Instead of asking them to make the sound of the rain, I organised the leaders to run around spraying the children with water bottles as the storm built up. It was very chaotic.

And throughout the talk, every time I held up a card with the words: 'You can't run away from God!' printed on it, the children had to shout out 'You can't run away from God!' They called out these words again and again and again.

This was the first talk given in a week long series of talks on Jonah. At the end of the week the children were asked by a visitor what they'd learnt from the book of Jonah. They called out, 'You can't run away from God!'

Why had they remembered word-for-word the point of the talk they'd heard at the beginning of the week, and not the talk they'd heard the day before? The point of the talk had been simply stated, and they had the job of repeating it again and again and again. When writing talks always ask – what can I get the children to do?

There is, however, one big problem in getting the audience to participate – adults.

The three rules to audience participation when adults are present (for example, in a church service) are:

1. Never ask adults to stand.
2. Keep adults seated at all times.
3. Under no circumstances ask adults to leave the safety of their seats.

Children love to move. They will stand up and yell at puppets. They will happily shout out to an actor on the stage. Adults, generally speaking, do not do these things. They like to sit. So audience participation needs to be thought through. As a general rule I invite adult participation but never enforce adult participation.

The mixed adult/child environment does restrict you. But please don't misunderstand me – children's talks in church, in the mixed adult/child environment are a great idea! Parents get to see what the children are learning.

A good children's talk will give parents the language with which to discuss ideas with their children. Children's talks should take huge concepts and reduce them to easy-to-remember phrases; phrases that can be picked up later and discussed. The other advantage is that adults and children learn together. When you teach the children chapter by chapter, section by section it is possible for you to work through the Bible as an entire church family.

This has been our practice for the past ten years. Whatever passage or topic the adults are working on – that's what we teach the children. It means that every part of the service is heading in the one direction. It also makes sense to teach the children within the context of the entire church family. Adults and children learn together.

Finally, how you present your talk is very important. Sometimes it seems as if we think, 'It's only kids'. We may not say it out loud, but every time we present a poor children's talk we shout it from the roof top.

Not every talk will work. You'll be able to judge whether you've done a good talk by the preparation you have put into it. Things may not all come together on the day, but if you have put in the work – prayed, studied the passage, worked on your script, asked for some feedback, practised it a number of times in front of a mirror or rehearsed it onto a tape – then before God and before you have even given the talk, it is a success. Try to value preparation more than presentation.

When our daughter Amy was four years old she loved the story of Cinderella. I would read her the story of Cinderella. I would tell the story of Cinderella. She would watch the video of Cinderella. She couldn't get enough of Cinderella.

One day as we were having afternoon tea together, Amy joined in the conversation on heaven by saying, 'I'm going to heaven'. My husband, Ray said, 'That's great Amy. Why is Jesus going to let you into his heaven?' To which Amy confidently replied, 'Because I'm a good girl!'

Ray stopped and thought for a moment then said, 'Amy, you know the story of Cinderella, but you don't know the full story'. Amy's eyes lit up as she knew a story was coming. Ray continued, 'Well, we know that Cinderella married the Prince. And when she came back from her honeymoon, because she was so very, very good, Cinderella invited her horrible stepsisters and stepmother to come and live with her. One day a preacher came to the palace. The preacher told everyone about Jesus; that he had died for them so that they could go to heaven. Well the stepsisters and the stepmother heard what the preacher said. They knew they were bad. They knew they needed to say sorry and to trust in Jesus. So they became Christians. But Cinderella thought she was good enough. Why she'd even let her mean stepsisters and stepmother come and live with her in the palace. So Cinderella refused to trust Jesus. She refused to say that she'd done anything wrong. And so God refused to let her come into his heaven.'

When Ray had finished Amy was devastated. She could not believe her ears – how could Cinderella not go to heaven? For the next hour she followed her father around arguing with him about his story. Ray did not present a three point argument. He simply entered into Amy's world and told a story to help her grow in her understanding.

Let us continue to work hard at retelling Jesus' stories in helpful ways to children. And let us work hard at finding new stories that challenge our children's thinking and faithfully teach them God's Word.

13.

PREACHING TO ADOLESCENTS

RICHARD NEWTON

Once upon a time there was a young man who was a youth group leader. He was soon to preach for the first time in church, something that both excited and frightened him. He really wanted to do it – and do it well. He had given some talks at youth group and camps, which seemed to have gone pretty well. However, on one occasion an opportunity for feedback was taken that would change his approach forever. It went something like this: 'Good talk ..., this was good ..., that worked ... etc ... but you could have done a bit more work on...' and the reply came back quickly and defensively, 'Oh yes, if this had been a "sermon" (he meant a talk in the regular church context) I would have worked it up a bit more'.

Does this shock you? Do you see the flaw in his defence? For those of you who don't, the reply then came back, 'Whether it's a sermon or a youth group talk, they are equally important, and must be treated as such'. It shocks me, that I could have thought that a youth group talk was not worthy of my effort, but to have verbalised it so brazenly, scares me. I recount the incident to you with thanks for the rebuke that I received, but also because I think it is a common mindset that exists when preaching to young people, often subconsciously, and it must be corrected.

The preparation process

The first and most important point on giving a talk to adolescents is that the process that you would go through for any talk, must be the same for a youth group talk – whether you are speaking to five fourteen-year-olds in your lounge room or speaking at a Christian youth convention. The process should be the same essentially, exegetically and prayerfully, giving glory to Jesus as Lord and Saviour.

If you are to be clear and helpful to those that you are serving, your 'big idea' must be what the 'big idea' of the passage is – if you are to teach them God's Word. It is tragic and all too common that people have the attitude that 'it's just a youth group talk'. If the talk is five or ten minutes long – a common scenario in the context of many youth events, it is essential that you work even harder to *nail* the 'big idea' and make the point clearly and quickly – not always as easy as it sounds – there is no room for rambling.

A typical youth group meeting on a Friday night when the leader has to give a talk might unfold like this. The leader has known he/she will have to give this talk all term, but the passage isn't even read until *that* day. After finishing work or Uni, and fatigued from a long week, he/she arrives home hoping to throw together a good biblically and theologically sound, engaging, life-changing talk in one hour, using a spent mind and tired body. This is to be repented of.

The importance of explaining God's Word in a comprehensive and comprehendible manner is paramount. This involves the preacher/teacher being careful and accurate with the Bible text in front of them, but also requires that they understand how to communicate and apply the truths to the specific audience they are speaking to.

In terms of dealing with the text properly and for some helpful preaching models, see other chapters in this book. The attention of this chapter will now turn to some specific points that are applicable to preaching to adolescents.

Bear in mind that the context will vary from churched to completely unchurched, formal to informal, voluntary to involuntary, young women to young men to a mixed group –

there are some helpful generalisations we can make about the uniqueness of adolescents that will impact on your preaching.

The uniqueness of adolescents
Put simply adolescence is the transition from childhood to adulthood, involving biological, cognitive and social development.[1]

Developmentally
During adolescence bodies change enormously, resulting in a heightened sense of body image consciousness. Cognitively, adolescents begin to think more abstractly. According to research they are also more idealistic, that is, they think about what is possible, thinking about ideal characteristics both for themselves and for others. Finally, adolescents become more logical, systematic and sequential than they were in childhood.[2]

Therefore, at a cognitive level it could be concluded that there is little difference in preaching to adolescents than to adults – at the level of an ability to comprehend, apprehend, analyse and apply information. Although this may be true in some cases, it would be a dangerous and unhelpful conclusion to apply. Since the reality is that in many contexts preaching takes place where there is an enormous spread of ages. Then there may well be those who at a cognitive level should be considered to be still in 'childhood' than adolescent stages. In addition, even with relatively narrow age spreads, there are often those who have developed far slower or faster than the majority. This complicates matters.

Given that adolescents are at a unique stage in life – physically, socially and cognitively – their hormones are doing crazy things. Does this alter our preaching to them? Of course, but I don't think that it means that we always preach on body image, sex, drugs and rock 'n' roll. Nor do I think that we flatten the landscape in terms of application to those areas. But I do believe it makes a difference in terms of understanding

---

[1] John W. Santrock, *Adolescence – An Introduction,* Brown and Benchmark Publications, Wisconsin, 5th edn, 1993, p 84.
[2] ibid. p. 122.

that at some point God's Word needs to be brought to bear on those issues. More than that though, is an understanding that there are significant changes and challenges facing the adolescent, which serve as distractions. Therefore, there is again a heightened need for clarity. One clear point, well applied and illustrated, driven by the text will be most helpful for the adolescent. This does not equate to lightweight or shallow talks – in fact I believe it means quite the opposite – there needs to be significant meat to a talk. Adolescents listen if they believe you have something to say, rather than just rambling on. The challenge is to avoid being shallow, and instead to be concise and challenging.

Environmentally and philosophically
Very rarely do adults find themselves in an involuntary context where they are exposed to the preaching of God's Word. This allows the preacher latitude that may not exist when preaching to adolescents. It is more likely that when adolescents are your audience they are there on an involuntary basis.

So what difference does this involuntary nature of your audience make? Since many of the audience are not present due to their own interest, curiosity or desire to become godlier as they sit under God's Word, the presentation must be even more punchy and easy to follow than in most adult contexts. By 'punchy' I mean that one clear point, made and driven by the text, must be made. If complex arguments are developed and listening becomes hard work, it is likely that many in the audience will be lost, disinterested and consequently left unchanged. Of course these are generalisations – and naturally there will be those who are motivated and stirred by the Holy Spirit regardless of how dry and complicated the talk is. The vested interest and therefore motivation of the voluntary listener of God's Word is, hopefully, the desire to know God and live for him. In these involuntary contexts where we often find ourselves preaching to the adolescent, this vested interest does not exist. Rather, it is something they have to do simply because of the school they attend, or as part of the family into which they have been born.

It is imperative to instil a vested interest in your listener. The adolescent's post-modern mindset is very different to that of previous generation's, giving them an altered view of the world; one that suggests that if you believe something – then that is right for you – but that absolute truth is neither attainable nor exists. Alternatively, they may not have formulated any idea of truth at all, or ever considered what they do or don't believe.

So it is with this firmly in mind that the preacher designs an opening question or scenario that is answered directly and precisely by the passage's 'big idea'. It should also include questions and issues that interest the adolescent. The preacher develops a vested interest by helping the hearer to see that the Bible and specifically the passage in front of them, is relevant and will challenge, correct or confirm their pre-conceived notions of the world and what the Bible says on particular subjects. Every attempt must be made to persuade, as Paul did in Corinth (Acts 18:4); to be invitational, not confrontational; to correct while being careful not to crush those with largely unconscious and underdeveloped worldviews.

Adolescents are less 'churched' than they used to be
In relation to the previous generation, this generation, (and I suspect following generations to a greater extent) are less and less 'churched'. Therefore, the prior knowledge of biblical concepts and theological terms must not be assumed. Simple explanations must be given and jargon avoided. Essential background must be given so that meaning may be comprehended. Again this emphasises the need for thorough preparation so that the complex may be made simple and digestible. Language that is outright churchy should be avoided – often this sort of language is not found in the text, so whether you think it is a vital theological term or not it should be avoided. Jargon ostracises people from the text itself, it does not aid in giving individuals confidence to read the Bible for themselves. This should be one of the aims for your young people – to be reading the Bible for themselves. If jargon such as 'justification' or 'sanctified' or 'sin' is used in the text, explain their meaning quickly and simply in non-

condescending language. You do not want to lose their minds in long-winded definitions from the dictionary.

Having said that the current generation of adolescents are largely unchurched, and therefore no knowledge can be assumed, many people still maintain that they know what the Bible teaches. The implication being, that when a passage is read and then explained, they will only hear the bits that confirm what they already believe. For example, many people might believe, 'God is happy with us when we do the right thing – whatever the right thing may be'. If you were giving a talk from Colossians 3:1-17, in verse 5 the imperative is concerned with living in a way that can rightly be described as being 'good'. However, the 'how to live' concerns the Christian, the person whose faith is in Christ (vv. 1-4 give the context, as v. 5 begins with 'therefore'). But the casual listener will hear 'live a good life'. Consequently, great care must be taken so that the gospel is not confused with good works. You need to be aware of what people hear – not just what you say. Anticipate the questions that arise from the text, but also anticipate what the audience may not pick up from the text and make those things particularly clear.

An external factor that will often be imposed on the preacher to adolescents, particularly in the formal contexts such as special school services such as Easter and Christmas and weekly chapel services, is that of time. Often the talk will have to be no longer than ten minutes, in some cases less. Therefore, there is little time to develop an argument, or establish theological treaties – you're in and out. You must keep to the point and be clear. Again, the hard work in preparation to keep distilling a talk down is essential. Keep sentences short and don't be wordy.

The compulsory attendance of your audience often creates the hyper-sceptic, of you and your message. For this reason it is even more essential to stick to the text. If you are clearly attempting to explain the Bible, there is a sense of objectivity involved. If you are just another authority figure 'ranting' at them – telling them what *you* think and how *they* should live, your message will lack power. After all, 'the word of God is living and active. Sharper than any double-edged sword, it penetrates even to dividing soul and spirit, joints and marrow; it judges the thoughts and attitudes of the heart' (Heb. 4:12). Given we are working with such a powerful, living and active Word, your conviction and passion should be compelling. Furthermore, they will judge you. Adolescents have an amazing ability to see through facades. They can tell when you are not being yourself. Be authentic – failure to do so will result in a loss of credibility, of you and your message. Do not attempt to be them. It may well be that you are similar culturally, that is fine, but don't pretend to be something you are not.

Do use material you know your adolescent audience will like, such as The Simpsons, sport or music. If you connect with them using subjects they enjoy, the hard things you say will be to a less-resistant hearer. For instance, recently at school we were preaching a series from Proverbs. The talk I was preparing was on the theme of 'the fool'. The audience was mostly non-Christian and I showed them a clip from the movie 'Jackass'. In the movie a series of stupid and sometimes dangerous acts are performed, such as riding a shopping trolley down a hill. The movie was used to draw the distinction between doing stupid but sometimes fun things, that is, being a Jackass, which has only a temporary consequence – and ignoring God, being a fool, which has an eternal consequence. I knew a lot of the boys at school had seen this movie, loved it, and talked about it. So as I was preparing, it came to mind. The movie made the point I wanted to make. It was enjoyed by the boys and gave me their attention. One important point as an aside is that it's not just 'adolescents' you must consider in your preparation, but the specific group you will speak too. This movie worked at a boy's school; it probably wouldn't have worked as well at a girl's school. Know your audience by listening hard to them. Critique their culture and use it to make your point without going overboard. You don't have to show the top of your underwear to connect!

There is something unique about adolescents and they do face fairly predictable issues, therefore the temptation is to always be preaching topically. The body image talk, the sex talk, the drugs talk, the ... talk. This is appropriate to an extent. Some topical talks will have an immediate connection, and not always be so predictable. Recently at the school I am a part of we had an evangelistic talk where attendance was not compulsory. The topic was rugby. It's a rugby school, the Rugby World Cup was being played in Australia – it was appropriate and it connected with the audience.

However, if we set our preaching agenda by what we think are the issues of the day we do our audience a disservice. This is because, firstly, we want our audience to be exposed to the whole counsel of God, as much as possible. This will not happen if we only choose to speak on topics. Secondly, we will not always know what the issues are and may miss the mark.

Conversely, if we systematically preach God's Word, the issues people face will in most cases be addressed, and from a God-centred perspective rather than an adolescent-centred perspective. Ideally our preaching will also model how to read the Bible on an individual basis. If we *only* ever preach topically, we will hamper this aim.

In his chapter on preparation, David Cook speaks of the 'dominant picture' in a passage. This is a very useful tool when applied to the preaching to adolescents – culturally and practically they are very visual. So ensure your language is descriptive and illustrations are vivid. The key is to ensure that the illustration is serving the text; not simply used because it was a 'good' illustration, or very funny and you 'had' to use it, or it impressed someone who you knew would be present. This is the temptation when you stand in front of teenagers; to spend a disproportionate amount of time on the illustration and leave inadequate time for a proper explanation of the text and its application. Illustrate, capture their minds, open them up – but do not get carried away with gimmicks or fun stories.

In conclusion, it must be said that much of the content of this chapter concerns preaching to the unbeliever. This is largely because the gap between preaching to the believing adolescent and adult is not as wide as to the unbelieving adolescent and adult. It is also uniquely the case that more unbelievers are preached to in this age group than believers. Adolescents are always filtering information, deciding what is relevant, and what can be discarded. Their worldviews are being largely formed at this stage of life. Whoever the audience, whatever their life stage, there is an urgency in their need for repentance and faith in Jesus; this alone will bring glory to God. Preaching that only consists of moral principles will not achieve this most vital obligation of every human being. Nor does any person have confidence in approaching the living Lord without them first having faith in Jesus. We must make this point our priority and to achieve our goal, certain principles should always apply. They are as follows:

- Prepare well
- Read widely
- Watch widely
- Observe carefully
- Listen well to adolescents
- Bring clarity – avoid wordiness/jargon/'churchiness'
- Be concise
- Be authentic, be yourself
- Know their issues – deal with them biblically
- Love them
- Explain the gospel
- Urge them to follow Jesus.

14

HOW TO PREPARE A BIBLE STUDY

Jenny Salt and Sue Steele-Smith

Why bother?
Imagine this . . .

- It's Wednesday night. The Bible study has been going for 45 minutes now. The group is up to question eight, the summary question. 'So, what's this passage all about?' ...But there's an awkward silence. George attempts to rephrase the question. The silence becomes even more pronounced.

- Karen has been leading the Bible study for a few months. Tonight's topic is 'The God we can trust in'. Karen takes the group to Jeremiah 29:11 and asks, 'What does this tell us about our God?' Sally brightly answers, 'God is going to prosper us and give us a great future. That's why I've been confident that I can wait for a good Christian man.' Karen feels her throat constrict. Somehow, she feels the answer is not quite correct. But she doesn't know why, and she doesn't know how to justify her thoughts.

- Peter has a brilliant study. It's immaculate, it's clean, the main idea is clear as crystal – but, he just noticed Jim yawning behind his hand. And Andy seems to have been eyeing off Erica... Peter is a bit perturbed. What's going on? Aren't they interested in the study?

Our poor Bible study leaders have some challenges, don't they?

- George's Bible study has been steadily sinking because he had no idea where he was heading when he wrote the questions.
- Karen didn't encourage her group members to study the passage in its context and so now she's out of her depth.
- Peter hasn't made any attempt to consider the individual learning styles of the group members. His study is polished but predictable, beautiful but boring.

These scenarios have provided good illustrations of why it is important to write Bible studies carefully! Preparing a good Bible study will take time. But it is worth persevering; because all Scripture is God breathed, it is living and active, able to rebuke, correct and encourage, and able to make people wise for salvation (Heb. 4:12, 2 Tim. 3:15, 4:2).

So what is critical in writing a good study? This chapter will address the essential elements of unpacking the text and then packaging the study.[1] As we work through this material, we will also demonstrate our method, step-by-step, by preparing a Bible study for you.[2] The study will focus on the well-known but often misunderstood narrative of David and Goliath, from 1 Samuel 17.

Imagine your Bible study leader informs you that he will be away in a month's time and he'd like you to take the study. Your group has been working systematically through 1 Samuel. Some studies have covered large chunks of text, for example, Chapters 4:1-7:1, whilst other studies have focused on a particular passage, for example, 1 Samuel 16:1-13. Your study will be looking at 1 Samuel 17. Where do you begin?

---

[1] We will assume that the passage has been chosen for you and your study is part of a series from a particular book of the Bible.

[2] This material is adapted from the Katoomba Youth Leadership Conference (KYLC) Strand material. We gratefully acknowledge the hard work of many KYLC committee members who have put this method together and refined it over the past 12 years.

PART A: Unpacking the Bible text
Let's start at the very beginning
Suppose you were studying a book about Einstein's theory of relativity. You would approach it quite differently from a text analysing Shakespeare's Hamlet! Similarly, this text would be very different from an essay critiquing Virginia Woolf from a postmodern perspective. We all know that when we approach any piece of text, if we want to come to grips with it, we need to understand its setting and its contents. It follows that in order to understand any Bible passage AND to write questions enabling others to understand it, you will also need to make a thorough investigation of the passage's context and subject matter. How do you do this?

Step 1: Getting started
To begin, you need to become familiar with the passage. Read, read and re-read. But – wait! Don't forget to pray before you start, and ask for God's insights through His Spirit (1 Cor. 2:12). Then, find a piece of paper and record some of your initial thoughts about the text. The following questions might help you.

- What seems interesting in this passage?
- What am I unsure about in this passage?
- What do I think the passage is all about?

Why don't you try this now with 1 Samuel 17? Some of our first impressions are recorded below.
- What seems interesting in this passage?
  The unevenness of the battle – the seasoned warrior versus the puny shepherd boy, but conversely the Lord versus those who defy him.
- What am I unsure about in this passage?
  Why didn't Saul know who David was, if David had already been playing the harp for him to soothe him?
- What do I think the passage is all about?
  At face value – God's faithfulness in giving victory to his people in overwhelming circumstances. Verses 45-47 outline the vindication of God's name in the face of his enemies.

Step 2: Digging deeper

Next, you have to dig deeper. What does the text say? What does the text mean? To investigate these things you will need to study both the 'context' and the 'contents' of the passage. The 'context' of your passage simply refers to its background. When studying any part of the Bible it is useful to investigate its literary, historical and theological contexts. The books of the Bible clearly don't all have the same literary style, nor were they all written under the same historical circumstances. Furthermore, when you are trying to understand a passage, you need to explore where it fits within God's revelation and what topics about God occur within it. By coming to grips with all three of these aspects of a passage's context, you will find more and more treasures packed within it.

Some useful questions to investigate these contexts are included below.

I. *Literary context*
   (i) What is the genre of my passage? That is, what type of literature is it? Is it a letter, a piece of historical narrative, a poem, a piece of advice (wisdom), a gospel, a parable, or apocalyptic? How does this genre influence the content of the passage?
   (ii) How does my passage fit in with the rest of the book?
   (iii) What ideas immediately precede and follow my passage?

II. *Historical context*
   (i) Who wrote the text? To whom? When was it written? When did the events occur?
   (ii) What was it written?

Sometimes the answers to these questions will be found in your passage. Sometimes the answers might be provided elsewhere within the book. At other times, you'll have no idea! In these cases it is helpful to go to a reliable commentary or Bible dictionary. But, as much as you can, try to avoid the commentaries until you've wrestled with the text yourself!

If you are working with a lengthy or confusing text, it can also be helpful at this stage to write a brief overview of the passage.

Why don't you try this with 1 Samuel 17? Photocopy and enlarge the blank Worksheet 1 (Appendix A) and complete the sections on historical and literary contexts. When you have completed this, look at our thoughts on the completed Worksheet 1 (In Appendix B). (Note: Try not to read ahead on our worksheet; you will benefit more by attempting to do this exercise yourself!)

III. *Contents*

It is helpful to look at the contents of your passage before investigating the theological context, because the two are always interrelated.

'Contents' refers to the words and structure of a particular passage. Which words seem important? Which words are repeated? How are these words related to one another? Can you identify any linking words (and, also, too), contrasting words (but, whereas, although, whilst), reason words (therefore, because, for, since, as, if, so), time words (when, next, after, then)? Can you see the role these words play within the text and its argument? Is there a clear structure in the passage? Can you follow the flow of thought through the text?

If possible, it is very helpful to make an enlarged photocopy of the passage. Then you can circle important words, draw arrows indicating connections between words, and write questions and miscellaneous thoughts around the text. As you investigate the contents of the passage, the following questions might be useful:

- Which words are repeated? Which words seem important? How are they related to each other?
- Are there significant linking, contrasting, reason or time words?

- Is there a movement of thought through the passage?

Why don't you try this now with 1 Samuel 17 and then look at our ideas? (Again, see Worksheet 1, Appendix B)

IV. Theological context

Finally, to interpret any Bible passage accurately, one must also investigate the theological context, that is, how the passage fits into the Bible's record of God's dealings with his people throughout history.[3] Where would you begin as you attempt to investigate how your passage fits into the Bible's overall message? The following outline will provide a starting point from which you can continue to write your study.[4]

(i)   Although the Bible is comprised of 66 books written by 40 different authors, it tells one unified story, as God works out his purposes of salvation for humanity.

(ii)   This story starts with a perfect creation (Gen. 1:31), which falls into sin (Gen.3), and concludes with God's promise of a new and perfect creation (Rev.2:10).

(iii) The key to understanding this story in its entirety is to see the life, death and resurrection of Jesus Christ as the central focus. Jesus was adamant that the whole of the Scriptures were written about him (John 5:29, Luke 24:44-47). Furthermore, when he commenced his public ministry, Jesus announced that the Kingdom of God was at hand. (Mark 1:14-15). The rest of the New Testament

---

[3] M. Strom, *Days are Coming*, Hodder & Stoughton, Rydalmere, 1989, p. 15.

[4] We recognise that a good understanding of biblical theology, that is, how the whole Bible testifies about Jesus, is critical to interpret any passage of the Bible correctly. Space prevents us from even attempting to address biblical theology in detail in this chapter. For further reading on biblical theology, see Graham Goldsworthy's *According to Plan* and Mark Strom's *Days are Coming*.

testifies to the fact that all of God's plans and promises for the establishment of his perfect kingdom are fulfilled in Jesus (2 Cor.1:20).

Hence, to understand a passage in its theological context, it is necessary to explore how it testifies to the crucial events of the gospel, and Jesus' part in God's Kingdom. It is only when this theological context has been explained that we can then consider what the passage might mean for us in our everyday lives.

Keeping all these ideas in mind, the following questions will help you to investigate your passage's theological context:

• What does the passage tell me about God (Father, Son or Spirit) and his purposes in this world?
• What does the passage tell me about God's Kingdom (people, place rule)?[5]
• Are there any verses in the passage quoted in other parts of the Bible?
• What significant Bible themes can I identify in the passage? (for example, temple, priesthood, sacrifice, prophet, rest). How are these ideas completed/fulfilled or transformed in Jesus?[6]

Why don't you try using these questions now with 1 Samuel 17 and then look at our ideas in Appendix B?

Step 3: The big idea
Well done for getting this far! The hard work has been done, now it is time to pull it all together. 'The big idea' is a short,

---

[5] Just as a kingdom is defined by a king ruling over his subjects in his sphere of dominion, the Kingdom of God can be described in terms of God's people under his perfect rule in his perfect place. This definition has been coined by Graeme Goldsworthy. For more details see *Gospel and Kingdom.*

[6] Don't panic if this terminology seems foreign! Depending on how much exposure you have had to biblical theology, these ideas might be new for you. If so, it would be beneficial to read *According to Plan.* The general idea is to investigate how this passage fits into the unfolding plan of salvation that finds its completion in Christ.

sharp summary sentence which captures the heart of the passage. (Remember George? He ran into problems because he had not identified his big idea.) Have a go now, and try to write a big idea for 1 Samuel 17.

As you were writing your big idea, did you feel as if it was incomplete? Was something missing? In view of the fact that the whole Bible is about Jesus, the big idea needs to reflect how your passage relates to Jesus. A helpful approach is to write your big idea, THEN write a second sentence showing how Jesus completed this idea.[7] Have a look at your big idea again and try to write that second sentence.

Discovering how Jesus fulfils the passage is a crucial step in your Bible study preparation. The Bible can be easily misinterpreted if we do not do this BEFORE we look at what the passage says to us. Remember Karen? Karen ran into difficulties because Sally tried to apply a text directly to herself. Instead, Karen should have helped Sally to understand how these ideas testified to Jesus before applying them personally.

Step 4: Applying the text – so what?
It is all very well to determine what the passage is saying – we could even give bonus points for explaining how Jesus completes the big idea! But what impact will this have on the members of our study group? There is one last stage in unpacking your text – application. The Bible always speaks to our everyday lives; we don't need to make it applicable. But unless you work hard at application, your Bible studies can tend to exist simply as interesting intellectual exercises. Good application questions will certainly help people to see how the Bible relates to them.

In order to apply your passage and ensure you have considered Jesus first, the following questions will be helpful at this stage of your preparation.

- How might this passage be misread if I don't look for the way that Jesus completes it? How did Jesus or any of the apostles apply this concept in the New Testament?

---

[7] See *According to Plan* to understand how the various parts of the Bible point to Jesus and how he completes biblical themes.

- How does the passage inform my beliefs? Do I need to change what I believe about God? Are there truths that I am encouraged to keep holding onto?
- How should this passage affect my behaviour? Is there anything I need to repent of? How should it change my thoughts, words and actions?

Think about the application for 1 Samuel 17 now, considering your group's specific needs and then have a look at our ideas in Appendix B.

Part B: Packaging the Bible study

Now that you have done the hard work of grappling with the passage, how are you going to present it so that your group will understand it and know how to put it into practice? Remember Peter? He had prepared a brilliant study but it didn't engage his group members. Why? Peter hadn't worked hard enough on packaging.

Packaging is definitely the easier part of your Bible study preparation. But it still requires thought, especially if you would prefer some variety! So what are the options for packaging?

1. Questions, questions, questions

The most common method of packaging is a series of inductive questions. These questions will help your group understand the context, contents and flow of the passage so that they can summarise the big idea, interpret it through Jesus, and then apply it to their own lives.

Most studies will include the following question types:
- A launching question tapping into the subject of the study.
- Questions which set the passage clearly within its context.
- Questions which investigate what the passage is saying – its contents.
- Interpretation questions which help people to think about what the text means.

- Summary questions. These are helpful as you move towards the big idea.
- A question which allows the group to explore how this passage is related to Jesus.
- Questions which enable the group to discover specific applications of this Scripture in their own lives, leading to repentance and growth in godliness.

2. How many questions?

Have you ever been in a Bible study where there are seemingly billions of questions? You are looking at the clock, thinking 'When is this going to end?' An important part of your packaging is to prepare the right number of questions to help people grasp the big idea without becoming bogged down in unnecessary detail. As a rough guide, for a 60-75 minute Bible study, you could start by working towards 10 questions covering the categories as suggested below.

- 1 launching question
- 1 context question
- 4 content questions
- 1 interpretation question
- 2 big idea / Jesus questions
- 1 application question

Of course this is only a rough guide. Sometimes you might need more interpretation questions or less content questions and so forth. Worksheet 2 in Appendix A can be photocopied and enlarged to help at this stage of your preparation.

3. BUT think outside the square! Creative packaging

If someone said 'Bible study' to you, what would you automatically think of? Most people think 'questions'! The question-answer style may be the only method of Bible study that you have ever seen, perhaps you've never thought about using any other method! But you can! In addition to questions and answers, there are other methods that can be used to explore Bible text creatively.

Educational psychologists recognise that people learn in many different ways. Some people are visual learners, others are auditory learners. Why not look for ways of engaging a variety of learning styles in your Bible study? Drawing, acting, interviewing, observing text together – this can be quite fun![8] Whilst it is possible to develop a whole Bible study around these creative learning methods, a great alternative is to use one such method to introduce the passage to your group members. Sometimes this will take the place of the launching question, and you can move directly into the rest of the study. For example, could you introduce your group to this passage by asking them to draw a picture, or getting them to do a role play? Perhaps you could break the group into halves and give them 10 minutes to set up a mock interview with some of the main characters.

Some space is provided on Worksheet 2 for those times when you want to use an alternative way into the study. Have a look at the completed worksheet to see an example using 1 Samuel 17. Our completed Bible study is then shown in Appendix C.

It's worth the bother!

Congratulations! You've worked through our method. Now you know how to write a Bible study. But perhaps you are thinking, 'Why bother with all this hard work? Why bother writing a Bible study when there are already so many out there to use?'

Certainly, you can save a lot of time if you use a pre-prepared study, but you won't understand the text as well as if you had worked through it yourself. You won't have benefited from it personally as much as when you do the hard work. Furthermore, some pre-prepared studies don't work hard enough at exploring the various contexts of the passage. But most importantly, a pre-prepared Bible study has been written for a generic audience. In contrast, when you write your own study you can gear it to your specific audience.

So is it worth the bother? As we conclude, cast your mind back to George, Karen and Peter. When you lead your Bible study do you want to know where the study is heading? Do you

---

[8] We want to acknowledge Karen and Rod Morris' *Leading Better Bible Studies*, Aquila Press, Sydney, 1997, for these ideas.

want to be confident that your members have understood what this passage means, considering its biblical context? Do you want to engage your group members, so that they are active, enthusiastic and ready to learn? Yes, preparing a Bible study is hard work, but yes, it is definitely worth the effort!

15.

How to prepare an evangelistic talk: the gospel, the people and the packaging

Ray Galea

1. The gospel

A. Preaching the gospel to oneself

To my shame I do not have a heart that is burdened for the lost. I remember sitting at the back of a bus with my friend Matthew who is a passionate evangelist. I asked, 'Matt, as you look on these people in the bus, mindful that most are without Christ, how does it affect you?'

He said, 'Ray, it upsets me deeply!'

My response was simply, 'It doesn't do a thing for me'.

As a result, I constantly have to tell myself why I preach the gospel and then pray like mad that I hold fast to those truths. Here are five reasons I keep on my prayer list to remind me why I preach the gospel.

Reason one: God's glory

We evangelise because we want God to be treated properly. We need to intentionally nurture a jealousy for God's glory. We want God's name to be hallowed and his will to be done on earth as it is in heaven. This must always be the first reason.

Reason two: Christ's compassion
We evangelise because of Christ's compassion. When Christ
saw the lost sheep of Israel (Matt. 9:35-38), his heart was filled
with compassion. His first instinct was to call on the disciples
to pray to the Lord of the harvest for gospel workers.

What liberated me from my lukewarmness was realising
that the lost matter to the Lord Jesus. It is why he came
(Luke 19:10). And if it matters to our Saviour then it must
matter to us!

Reason three: The destiny of the lost
At times I do have a clarity that is not with me from day to day.
There are moments when I ponder the holy wrath of God and
the fate of the lost. So before we preach to others we must
meditate on what is at stake for those who don't receive Christ.
Sometimes we have to put the hard word on ourselves.

Reason four: My own encouragement
It is such a thrill to see God at work. It is an honour that God
would use 'shmucks' like us to bring in the elect. In the words
of 1 John 1:4, 'It makes my joy complete'.

Reason five: Under orders!
If Timothy was under orders to 'Do the work of an evangelist'
(2 Tim. 4:5) then I as a pastor/teacher am under no less
a compulsion from my King.

B. Gospel preaching is preaching the Lord Jesus
Gospel preaching is about preaching the good news concerning
the Lord Jesus Christ. There is nothing like stating the
obvious!

In Romans 1:3 the Apostle Paul tells us that God's gospel
is about his Son. It is captured in the very name and title
'Jesus the Christ'. The personal name of Jesus simply means
'Yahweh saves'. As the angel told Joseph '...you are to give him
the name Jesus, because he will save his people from their
sins' (Matt. 1:21). The title 'the Christ' refers to the promised
anointed King whom God would give to the nations as his
inheritance. At its heart the gospel is about Christ's saving

kingship. In its briefest form the gospel is Christ Jesus our Lord.

In 1 Corinthians 15:1-5 Christ's saving Lordship climaxes in his sin-bearing death and death-destroying resurrection as the fulfilment of Scripture.

As Gospel preachers, whatever we do, whatever we say, it is not until we proclaim the saving Lordship of Christ that we are 'gospelling'. There is a place for pre-evangelistic talks, but they must not be confused with evangelistic preaching. Why am I stating the obvious? One of the men in my congregation is involved in promoting the gospel at his work place. One minister he invited to speak never mentioned the name Jesus. The following speaker, who was specifically asked to give an evangelistic message, decided instead to give a talk on leadership. However, what really discouraged my friend was that the rest of the Christians at his work place failed to see the problem. If the preacher is not clear on the gospel, neither will the congregation be clear. We can talk all we like about subjects such as the Church, the Spirit, God's guidance, abortion, healing, and predestination; but we are only preaching the gospel when we are proclaiming Christ's saving Lordship.

The right response to the gospel is faith and repentance, based on the logic of who Jesus is. Since Jesus is Lord, the response must be repentance, and since Jesus is Saviour, the response is one of faith.

Though faith and repentance are not part of the gospel itself, we should not preach Christ crucified without calling for a response.

C. Preaching the gospel from the Scriptures
Wherever possible, we ought to preach the gospel from the Scriptures. Paul says in 2 Timothy 3:15 that the Holy Scriptures, '... are able to make you wise for salvation through faith in Christ Jesus'.

If that is their purpose then let us preach Christ Jesus as Lord from the Bible. This will not always be appropriate at certain outdoor events or dialogue meetings. What is often required in such contexts are short and sharp gospel pre-sentations.

There is an air of integrity in what we do when we strive to show from where our gospel comes. It is a gospel that is received before it is passed on. It is received from Christ through his apostles via the Scriptures.

The other advantage is that we avoid presenting the gospel truths in the same predictable format. Beware of preaching a tightly defined gospel format which is imposed on each passage. Let the nuances of the text shape the presentation.

If we preach the gospel always using the same idioms and illustrations, our congregation will begin to be contemptuous at the sheer predictability of this awesome gospel. They will be less likely to bring friends, and more likely to stay away themselves.

D. Preaching the text in context

The power of the gospel does not rely on the great illustrations we have up our sleeve. I've often fallen into this trap. Rather the power is found in Jesus' saving Lordship as he is revealed in the Scripture.

Preparing an evangelistic talk is essentially the same as preparing a sermon for the saints. The normal rules of reading the Bible in context operate (see relevant chapter). Of special note, when preaching from the Gospels the one context we must not forget is that of Christ's death and resurrection.

Where evangelistic preaching is different from other preaching is that we are:

a) Totally focused on the non-Christian, and
b) Assuming much less from the listener, for example, Bible-knowledge.

2. The People

Know the people to whom you preach the gospel

Evangelistic preaching is highly sensitive to the mindset of the non-Christian listener. However such sensitivity must not alter the gospel.

It is clear that Paul has his audience constantly in mind when he preaches as well as when he writes his letters. A simple comparison between Paul's preaching to the Jews at Pisidian Antioch (Acts 13) and to the Gentiles in Athens (Acts 17) highlights this point. The Apostle shapes his address to his audience, without ever altering the heart of the gospel.

In preaching the gospel effectively we must know how our listeners think. Though slightly dated, a poem by British journalist, Steve Turner, entitled 'Creed', still speaks to the mindset of many to whom we preach. To see this poem, go to: www.apuritansmind.com/Apologetics/SteveTurnerCreed.htm

The beauty of this poem is that it allows us to enter into the attitudes of the modern western mind. It is crucial to know the worldview of the people we are speaking to for the following reasons:

- We need to know the philosophical world of our listeners. Steve Turner's poem captures some of the humanistic relativism of our age. Make sure that you are answering the questions that people are asking.
- We need to know how worldviews are promoted in popular culture. Most people live in a world fed by television sitcoms, Hollywood films, songs, glossy magazines and talkback radio. Some people preach like they live on another planet.
- We need to be aware of how people operate at a personal level. Most individuals are caught up with the immediate: family relationships, fears, grief, unemployment, raising the kids and wondering whether they will ever marry or remarry.
- We all, and particularly male preachers, need to recognise when the audience is male and female. When illustrating, some preachers never get beyond football stories.
- We need to know the theology of our audience. As a culture we may be post-Christian, but there is still a remnant of teaching on God, Jesus, sin, salvation, heaven and hell, influenced by Sunday school, youth groups, church and tele-evangelists.
- Most importantly we need to pay attention to the specific subculture we are dealing with. While postmodernism

covers our urban Australian landscape, for me living in the western suburbs of Sydney, among a high percentage of working class middle-easterners, I am preaching to a modernist mindset.

When all is said and done, if we really want to understand people, there is no substitute for spending time talking to them personally about Jesus. This gives us a real opportunity to hear how people actually think. The gospel is never preached in a vacuum and we have to understand the people we are trying to reach.

To illustrate how we seek to understand our audience, let's explore the interface between the world and Mark 2:1-12, which is an ideal passage for gospel preaching.

Non-Christian assumption	Mark 2:1-12 assumption
God: Exists for most yet often thought of as the insipid 'man upstairs.' More harmless than dangerous.	God: He is the aggrieved holy judge, whose wrath is to be feared. Yet whose mercy is found in Jesus' authority to forgive sin.
Judge: Conscience.	Judge: God.
Guilt: An emotion one feels.	Guilt: A verdict of condemnation that will culminate in judgment on the last day.
Sin: If mentioned only refers to serious grievances towards other humans e.g. paedophilia, ethnic gang rape or CEO's salary packages. None of which are able to be forgiven.	Sin: Rebellion against a personal God, for which each person is held responsible.
Salvation: Learning to forgive oneself.	Salvation: God no longer counting our sins against us.

There is clearly a growing loss of shared assumptions between the western world and the Bible. As we proclaim Christ we need to be aware that we are teaching new and often offensive ideas. We are often correcting misunderstandings and caricatures. We are directly challenging deep-seated presuppositions. While such teaching needs to be done respectfully and engagingly, the truth needs to be stated outright.

Paul certainly began his sermon at the Areopagus inclusively by beginning where the listeners were at ('to an unknown god'). He positively quoted their poets and used inclusive language. However, the Apostle ended on the exclusive note that God '... commands all people everywhere to repent' (Acts 17:30).

The bridge between God's Word and the world is to teach the gospel and its assumptions. Failure to do so will result in a pleasant but incomplete Jesus who offers a therapeutic salvation, in which a person can simply learn to live at peace with themselves.

3. THE PACKAGING OF A GOSPEL SERMON
Let us now consider the various elements of an evangelistic talk. It is helpful at the beginning to flag with the listeners that you will call on people to make a commitment to Christ. It prepares the listeners to make a more informed decision. The sermon is not just another story to be shared. It also allows people to listen more actively because a response is anticipated.

A. Opening prayer
Do we begin a gospel sermon with public prayer? It depends on the context. If your venue is a university bar, then no; if it is a Sunday morning outreach service, then probably yes. The answer will depend partly on the expectation of the audience. Prayer should not present a stumbling block.

How do we pray? The one value that is common to western humanity is a desire to be open-minded. Hence I tend to pray a prayer for open-mindedness. Since we are leading non-Christians in prayer, address God as 'God', not as Father.

B. Introduction
The function of an introduction is to introduce the big idea of the passage. Its aim is to provoke a desire to want to know more. This is the point of entry for the gospel. It is where

we make links between God's Word and their world. The introduction is the point of contact between God's story and their story. Remember, we are not making Jesus relevant but showing how he is already relevant.

State your opening point explicitly in short punchy language. The introduction has the advantage of further introducing you as a person. Don't assume they want to listen. The onus is on the speaker to make the connections in an engaging manner. Do not hide the power of God's Word behind sloppy introductions.

For more information on effective introductions, please see Chapter 6.

C. Body of the talk

In essence you preach the gospel by expounding the text and applying it to your listeners. If you lack clarity, bind yourself to a structure. Here is a helpful structure given by John Chapman:

a) State the point
b) Show the point from the Bible
c) Explain the point
d) Illustrate the point
e) Apply the point

Other issues to keep in mind:
Expounding the Bible is the hardest kind of preaching to do and the easiest to bore people with.

(i) *Wisely edit your sermons.* Be aware of length and what is manageable for the hearer. The mark of a good sermon is what is left on the cutting room floor. Sermons tend to fail in two areas:

- they either tell us more than we are able to grasp, or
- they don't tell us enough and fail to sufficiently engage with the text.

Try to cover the key territory without being overly technical. For example, when preaching on Mark 2:1-12, I don't refer to the Daniel 7:13 background for the 'Son of Man' title when my prime focus is on the outsider.

(ii) *Turn theological ideas into plain English.* It is crucial to make the complex simple. I remember preaching evangelistically on Mark 8:27ff, where Peter declares that Jesus is 'The Christ'. I had a full page on what the term 'Messiah' meant and went into great detail from 2 Samuel 7 and Psalm 2. John Chapman later said to me, 'Why don't you just say, "If a person's name is John, his title is plumber and his job description is to fix taps. In the same way Jesus is his name, his title is Christ which means King and his job description is to rule the world"?'

(iii) *Deal simply with theological difficulties.* In Mark 2:9 Jesus poses the question, 'Which is easier: to say to the paralytic, "Your sins are forgiven," or to say, "Get up, take your mat and walk"?' You can spend a lot of time answering that question. I simply state, 'Both are impossible for us and both are possible for God'.

(iv) *We function like mediators when we preach.* On the one hand we need to sympathise with the listener's reaction to the hard edges of God's Word. Yet at the same time we ultimately side with God. What do I mean by sympathize with the people? For example, when it comes to the question of hell, I want to say that 'it does feel like the punishment seems to exceed the crime'. Yet at the same time I don't want to sound like I am apologising for hell. So I also want to say that my own reaction tells me how little I understand both the seriousness of my sin and the holiness of God.

(v) *Think through the positive aspects of each doctrine.*
Here are two examples.

- The Day of Judgment means that in a meaningless world I matter and so does God.

- Sin means that when I am on the receiving end of other people's abuse there is someone other than me taking my side.

(vi) *Expose the clichés of our world.* Clichés carry the theology of the average person. It is up to us to expose them in the light of the biblical truth.

Cliché: We believe that everything is getting better.
Critique: Despite evidence to the contrary.
Cliché: We believe that all religions are basically the same.
Critique: They only differ on matters of creation, sin, heaven, hell, God and salvation...

(vii) *Find the language and images that translate the gospel doctrines into familiar categories.* When Paul expounds 'justification by faith' in Romans 4:5 he says, 'However, to the man who does not work but trusts God who justifies the wicked, his faith is credited as righteousness'. What do Australians call a person who chooses not to work? Everyone always gives me the same answer, 'Bludger'. The Australian equivalent would be, 'Unless you're prepared to bludge on the mercy of God you will never be forgiven'.

(viii) *Quote the world to defend the truth as Paul does in his sermon in Athens.* All truth is God's truth and it is sometimes easier to hear the truth from an outsider. For example, in Bob Dylan's song, entitled *The Disease of Conceit* he writes, 'Whole lot of people seeing double tonight from the disease of conceit. Give ya delusions of grandeur and an evil eye, Give you the idea that you're too good to die'.

D. Conclusion
The conclusion has one aim – that is to call for faith and repentance. It is crucial that you use words consistent with the language of the text and the sermon. The conclusion is not the time to introduce new ideas. It is the time to address the will.

Too many preachers are afraid to directly call on people to commit, and to commit to Christ now! We need to get over our hesitation! Keep in mind that it is ultimately God who is calling people through the gospel that leaves our lips. So speak accordingly with a sense of urgency.

Preaching is not simply imparting information. It is about earnestly persuading the listener to bow before the Lord Jesus and warning them of the consequences if they do not repent. We must not get so sophisticated that we forget that our listeners are under God's wrath. This may be their last opportunity to repent. I remember driving while on holidays and watching the car in front of me veer on to the other side of the highway. I assumed the driver had fallen asleep. All I had was my horn, which I blasted the daylights out of in order to wake the driver from his micro sleep. It worked and the car went back on the right side of the road. Never forget that ours is a warning ministry.

One of the biggest reasons people have for not coming to Christ is the cost of commitment. So help them count the cost and realise that it is nothing compared to the cost of missing out on Christ. If you don't call for faith and repentance, you will give the impression that judgment day is like a quiz show where faith is having the right answer, such as, 'Jesus died for my sins'.

If through your expounding of the passage, the Lordship of Jesus has not been clearly emphasised, then make sure you emphasise it before you call on them to pray the prayer.

E. Closing prayer

The most helpful and, it seems to me, the most natural way to lead a person to Christ is to lead them in a prayer to their Father in heaven. The purpose of the prayer is to express their new found trust, in words to God. When you lead them in the prayer, say it slowly enough for the person to repeat it quietly in their own mind to God. And tell them that is what you are doing. Make sure your prayer uses the words picked up in the sermon and the Bible passage.

The prayer should include:

- A confession of sin,
- A thankful trust in Jesus' death and resurrection, and
- A commitment to submit to Jesus as Lord and Saviour.

After the prayer has been prayed, point out the blessings that flow from a genuine faith and express the joy felt by both heaven and earth in having one sinner who repents.

It is crucial that those who prayed the prayer and those who want to know more are offered the opportunity to be followed-up. Getting people to fill out a confidential card is, I believe, the best method of follow up. Remember the best work will happen in an ongoing follow-up Bible study in fellowship with other Christians.

Remember that most of the work happens AFTER the sermon. Make sure you give them the opportunity to give you their details for follow-up. And don't forget, after you have wiped the sweat from your brow, as you see another person come into the kingdom, remember that it is God who grants repentance, and so thank him for allowing you to be his co-worker.

'But you, keep your head in all situations, endure hardship, do the work of an evangelist, discharge all the duties of your ministry' (2 Tim. 4:5).

APPENDIX A

BIBLE STUDY PREPARATION - WORKSHEET 1

PASSAGE: _____

Overview

Context and Content
1. Literary context

2. Historical Context

3. Content

4. *Theological Content*

- What does my passage tell me about God and how he does things?

- AND/OR ... What does it tell me about God's Kingdom? (God's people, God's place and God's rule)

Big Idea

- Big Idea

- Completed in Christ

Implications

- Jesus/NT (how NT runs with this idea)

- Beliefs (keep holding, adjust)

- Behaviour (change, repent)

BIBLE STUDY PREPARATION – WORKSHEET 2

TEXT_____ TITLE _____

Big Idea

Creative Packaging

Launch
1.

Context
2.

Content
3.

4.

5.

6.

Interpretation
7.

Summary (Big Idea and Jesus)
8.

9.

Implications
10.

11.

APPENDIX B

PASSAGE: 1 SAMUEL 17

Overview

Battle between army of Israel and Philistines; Defiant Goliath defeated; David victorious; the Lord saves; the Lord's name is vindicated.

(1-10)	Philistines and Goliath
(11-24)	David
(25-40)	The Israelites
(41-51)	The battle
(52-58)	The aftermath

Context and content

1. Literary context
- Chapter 17 follows
  Saul, first King of Israel, Chapter 10, continuing battle with Philistines, disobedience of Saul and rejection by the Lord (ch. 15),
  David anointed by Samuel (ch. 16 note 16:7), then David plays harp for Saul
- Chapter 17 precedes:
  Saul's reaction to David's success, jealousy and murder plot (ch. 18)
  Saul dies in battle and David reigns over united Israel (2 Sam.)

2. Historical Context

Narrative events set during reign of Saul (~1040 BC–1000 BC)
Author unknown
Date of writing: Different views? After Babylonian exile or near end of David's reign?

3. Content

- Repeated words/themes
    - defy (10, 25, 26, 35, 45)
    - shrinking back, running forward
  Army of Israel shrinking back, David running forward towards Goliath
  Philistines running away, Israelite army pursuing enemy
- Length of speeches
  Goliath and David (41-47) contrast with short description of actual battle and defeat (48-50)
- Significant verses (46-47)
- Movement of thought – weakness vs strength
    - weakness of Israel, King
    - strength of Philistines, Goliath
    - weakness of David, younger brother, too small for King's armour
    - strength of Israel's God, 'battle is the Lord's'
- Contrast attitudes of Saul, Israelites, David to see David's insights into the situation

4. Theological Content

- What does my passage tell me about God and how he does things?
  God's purpose: to be known (46) and to save (47)
  God: powerful to save (47)
  God doesn't act in the way the world acts, uses weakness to reveal his power
- AND/OR ... What does it tell me about God's Kingdom? (God's people, God's place and God's rule)
  God's people: David, the unlikely victor whose confidence remains in the Lord contrasted with other Israelites who

lack faith, stand by and see the victory won on their behalf

God's place: not significant here

God's rule: God still the living, vastly superior God, battle belongs to him, saves but not by sword or spear

Summary: Emphasis on God's victory using unlikely hero

Big idea

- Big idea
  God saves his people Israel through the weakness of his chosen one, David
- Completed in Christ
  Points forward to time when God would save all his people from a bigger enemy (sin and death) through his chosen one, Jesus, and foolishness of his weapons, the cross. (Note: Who should we identify with – David? Or the Israelites who stood by and watched the victory won on their behalf?)

Implications

- Jesus/NT (how NT runs with this idea)
  1 Cor. 1:18-25 Power of God seen in weakness, God used the weak things of this world to shame the wise, 'message of the cross is foolishness'
  1 Cor. 15:54-57 Death has been swallowed up in victory
- Beliefs (keep holding, adjust)
  God saves through the weakness of the cross – thank him!!
  God's name is to be honoured and not defied
  Vast superiority of my God over any of his opponents
- Behaviour (change, repent)
  Concern for the honour of God's name in my own life and the life of others
  No arrogance e.g. 'God will simply do this for me'

Bible Study Preparation – Worksheet 2

Title: The Big Baddie and the Weak Winner

Text: 1 Samuel 17

Big Idea
God saves his people Israel through the weakness of his chosen one, David
God saves through his chosen one, Jesus Christ, through the weakness of the cross

Creative Packaging
Divide into three small groups and ask each group to set up an interview with one of the following key people in the narrative. Some sample questions are provided although each group might think of their own questions.

Key people:
Saul (and the Israelites)
Goliath (and the Philistines)
David the shepherd boy

Interview with Saul
- How did you feel when Goliath repeatedly challenged and defied your army?
- How did you come to meet David on the battlefield and what were your first impressions of him?
- Why were you convinced that he could fight Goliath?

Interview with Goliath
- What was your impression of the battle situation at Socoh?
- What were your first impressions of David as he came out to fight you?
- Why didn't you take him seriously?

Interview with David
- What were you thinking when you first heard Goliath's defiant challenge to the Israelite army?
- What did you and King Saul talk about when you were taken to him?
- Why were you so confident that you could fight Goliath?

Following the interviews, ask the following question:

From these interviews, what would you identify as the main concern in Chapter 17?

Launch
1. No launch – creative packaging instead.

Context
2. What was Saul like when he was first appointed King? (1 Sam. 10:24) What is he like now? (16:14, 23; 17:11)

Content
3. Describe the enemy (17:4-10, 41-44). What word describing his attitude is constantly repeated in the narrative? (10, 36) In spite of his taunts, how powerful were his gods? (43 cf. 51-53)

4. How did the Israelites react to Goliath (11, 24) and where did their interests lie? (25)

5. Despite his youth and lack of weapons, David was very confident about victory. Where did his confidence lie? Look at his conversation with both the Israelites (26, 37) and Goliath (45, 46, 47).

Interpretation
6. Why was David an unlikely choice as the one who came and rescued Israel? (15, 33, 38-40)

7. The outcome of the battle is, of course, that David triumphed over the Philistines (50). What happened to make this possible? (46-47) Who is the main focus of this battle?

Summary (Big idea and Jesus)

8. What does this fight between David and Goliath tell us about the way God works?

9. David's victory over Goliath reminds us of another unlikely Saviour, King David's greater Son, Jesus. Compare these saviours, their enemies and the weapons they used. (1 Cor. 1:18-25; 15:54-57)

Implications

10. How does this story relate to the way God works today? Just as David defeated Goliath, should we expect that God will help us to win the sometimes overwhelming daily battles of life? Why or why not?

11. How will you live today, in view of God's victory won at the cross? Consider these scenarios: At work, how will you react if someone makes an offensive joke about God? What do we mean when we pray 'hallowed be your name' in the Lord's Prayer? Do you expect God to answer that prayer? In your devotional times, are you reminding yourself of the wonder of salvation through Christ crucified?

APPENDIX C

The Big Baddie and the Weak Winner

1 Samuel 17

Introduction:
Divide into three small groups. Each group is to interview one of the key people in the narrative. (Your leader will give you some interview questions, although you might think of your own.)

Key people:
  Saul (and the Israelites)
  Goliath (and the Philistines)
  David the shepherd boy

From these interviews, what do you identify as the main concern of Chapter 17?

We see in this familiar story an amazing picture of victory against overwhelming odds. But is it simply about the 'Goliaths' we are facing and the 'stones' we can use to overcome, or is there more to it?

1. Enter Saul
What was Saul like when he was first appointed King? (1 Sam. 10:24) What is he like now? (16:14, 23; 17:11)

2. *Enter Goliath*
Describe the enemy (17:4-10, 41-44). What word describing his attitude is constantly repeated in the narrative? (10, 36) In spite of his taunts, how powerful were his gods? (43 cf. 51-53)

3. *Enter the Israelites*
How did the Israelites react to Goliath (11, 24) and where did their interests lie? (25)

4. *Enter David*
Despite his youth and lack of weapons, David was very confident about victory. Where did his confidence lie? Look at his conversation with both the Israelites (26, 37) and Goliath (45-47)

5. Why was David an unlikely choice as the one who came and rescued Israel? (15, 33, 38-40)

6. The outcome of the battle is, of course, that David triumphed over the Philistines (50). What happened to make this possible? (46-47) Who is the main focus of this battle?

7. What does this fight between David and Goliath tell us about the way God works?

8. David's victory over Goliath reminds us of another unlikely Saviour, King David's greater Son, Jesus. Compare these saviours, their enemies and the weapons they used. (1 Cor. 1:18-25, 15:54-57).

9. How does this story relate to the way God works today? Just as David defeated Goliath, should we expect that God will help us to win the sometimes overwhelming daily battles of life? Why or why not?

10. How will you live today, in view of God's victory won at the cross? Consider these scenarios: At work, how will you react if someone makes an offensive joke about God? What do we mean when we pray 'hallowed be your name' in the

Lord's Prayer? Do you expect God to answer that prayer? In your devotional times, are you reminding yourself of the wonder of salvation through Christ crucified?

LIST OF CONTRIBUTORS

Rev Dr Sam Chan
Prior to his theological training at Sydney Missionary and Bible College (SMBC), and the Trinity Evangelical Divinity School in Chicago, Sam practised medicine. At SMBC, Sam lectures in preaching, ethics and theology. He is ordained in the Chinese Christian Fellowship Church. Sam's PhD examined speech act theory in the area of preaching.

Canon John Chapman
John is an evangelist who, before retiring, worked with the Anglican Church in Sydney. The author of many books including *A Fresh Start* and *Know and Tell the Gospel*, John has taught evangelism at Sydney Missionary and Bible College and Moore Theological College.

Rev David Cook
David is Principal of Sydney Missionary and Bible College. After graduating from SMBC and Moore Theological College, he served as a Presbyterian minister in country and city parishes. David lectures in preaching and pastoral subjects, and speaks at Christian conferences in Australia and overseas. His books include *The Unheeded Christ* and *Teaching Acts*.

Rev Stuart Coulton
Stuart is the Pastoral Vice-Principal at Sydney Missionary and Bible College. Stuart practised law before spending 15 years in parish ministry. At SMBC he lectures in church history, pastoral care and theology and has had extensive involvement with Katoomba Christian Conventions in Australia.

Mr Jonathan Dykes
Jonathan is the Associate Director of the Sydney Missionary and Bible College School of Preaching. Prior to this role, Jonathan gained wide experience in preaching though parish work, and an evangelistic ministry to business workers in Sydney. He lectures at SMBC in preaching subjects and is a regular preacher at Christian conventions.

Bishop Dudley Foord
Dudley has a lifetime of pastoral, chaplaincy and teaching experience as well as holding doctorates in ministry and divinity. He served as Bishop of the Church of England in South Africa in the 1980s. In recent years Dudley has worked as a consultant in evangelism and church ministries.

Rev Ray Galea
Ray is the pastor of the Multicultural Bible Ministry, an Anglican church in Sydney's western suburbs. He ministers particularly to second generation Mediterranean and Middle Eastern people in that area. Ray is also a visiting faculty member for the SMBC School of Preaching. His book *Nothing in My Hand I Bring* was recently published in Sydney.

Mrs Sandy Galea
Sandy has extensive experience teaching children at church (where she works with her husband Ray), through Christian camping, kids' clubs and beach missions. She also trains children's workers. Sandy has written hundreds of children's talks. Her book, *Children's Talks – A Practical Guide* (SMBC Press), shares insights from her work.

Rev Simon Manchester
Simon is the senior minister of a large Anglican church in North Sydney. He can also be heard preaching regularly on a popular Sydney radio station, and writes for several Christian journals. Simon is a well-known conference speaker throughout Australia and overseas.

Rev Richard Newton
Richard is school chaplain at The Armidale School, a large Anglican boys' high school in northern New South Wales.

Prior to studying at Sydney Missionary and Bible College he worked as a schoolteacher. For some years Richard has directed the high school youth programmes at Katoomba Christian Conventions.

Ms Jenny Salt
As Dean of Women, Jenny is responsible for the pastoral care of single women at Sydney Missionary and Bible College. She is also on the faculty of the School of Preaching, with a particular emphasis on training women. Jenny regularly speaks at women's events and conferences throughout Australia.

Ms Sue Steele-Smith
Sue lectures in church history and Christian education at Sydney Missionary and Bible College. Previously, she worked in full time parish ministry with women, children and overseas students at a Presbyterian church in Sydney. Sue has an educational background, having taught science and English as a second language.

Rev Grant Thorp
Grant is the senior minister at Randwick Presbyterian Church in Sydney and has also pastored churches in rural New South Wales. He is also a well-known speaker at Christian conventions throughout Australia. Grant is a visiting faculty member in the Sydney Missionary and Bible College School of Preaching.

Dr Leigh Trevaskis
Leigh holds a doctorate in veterinary science from Sydney University, and a Master of Divinity through Sydney Missionary and Bible College. He is currently completing a PhD in Old Testament, and following that will join the faculty at Queensland Theological College .

TEACHING ACTS

Unlocking the book of Acts
for the Bible Teacher

DAVID COOK

SERIES EDITORS: DAVID JACKMAN & ROBIN SYDSERFF

PROCLAMATION
TRUST MEDIA

Teaching Acts

Unlocking the book of Acts for the Bible Teacher

David Cook

Published in conjunction with the Proclamation Trust.

There are commentaries, and there are books on preaching – but very few books that enable the preacher or Bible teacher to prepare and present a series on specific sections of scripture.

This series complements commentaries by giving Bible teachers suitable tools to understand the context of Biblical books; doctrinal themes; the methods of interpretation; the key teaching points and how to deliver that message to the audience.

Whilst very useful for preachers, the book is also aimed at enabling youth workers and small group study leaders have the confidence they need to teach Biblical principles and doctrine.

Teaching Acts takes the book of the Acts of the Apostles and enables the leader to explain the context of the early formative days of the church and the application of practical theology to specific situations that still affect the church today.

David is the Principal and Director of the School of Preaching at Sydney Missionary and Bible College.

ISBN 978-1-84550-255-3

Christian Focus Publications

publishes books for all ages

Our mission statement –

STAYING FAITHFUL
In dependence upon God we seek to help make His infallible Word, the Bible, relevant. Our aim is to ensure that the Lord Jesus Christ is presented as the only hope to obtain forgiveness of sin, live a useful life and look forward to heaven with Him.

REACHING OUT
Christ's last command requires us to reach out to our world with His gospel. We seek to help fulfil that by publishing books that point people towards Jesus and help them develop a Christ-like maturity. We aim to equip all levels of readers for life, work, ministry and mission.

Books in our adult range are published in three imprints.
Christian Focus contains popular works including biographies, commentaries, basic doctrine and Christian living. Our children's books are also published in this imprint.
Mentor focuses on books written at a level suitable for Bible College and seminary students, pastors, and other serious readers. The imprint includes commentaries, doctrinal studies, examination of current issues and church history.
Christian Heritage contains classic writings from the past.

Christian Focus Publications, Ltd
Geanies House, Fearn, Ross-shire,
IV20 1TW, Scotland, United Kingdom
info@christianfocus.com

www.christianfocus.com